Macon H. Hare

THE GROWTH OF THE IDEA OF GOD

THE GROWTH OF THE IDEA OF GOD

BY

SHAILER MATHEWS, D.D., LL.D.

DEAN OF THE DIVINITY SCHOOL OF THE
UNIVERSITY OF CHICAGO

59

NEW YORK
THE MACMILLAN COMPANY
1931

TO
MY WIFE

PREFACE

MY purpose is not so much to give an exhaustive study of religion as to show how the idea of God has developed in Western civilization. For this reason I have not thought it necessary to enter into any elaborate discussion of primitivity. There are admirable works in that field wherein those interested can find an immense amount of information about the practices of primitive people the world over. To my mind the development of the idea of God is more important than its origin. It is its own answer to the charge that religion is superstition. Religious thought and practices are as necessary as economic, political, or scientific. And among the developed religions Christianity is unique in that it not only is a religion within our own civilization but its development for 3,000 years or more is well documented. In so far as other religions have moved toward monotheism their history is valuable for purposes of comparative study. Their divergencies as well as their similarities are illuminating. The one great prerequisite for an understanding of the development of the idea of God is that one shall be historically and socially minded. We have in religion not a speculation but the actual experience and hopes of men. Did not defense or criticism of theism so frequently ignore or misuse history and sociology, it would seem to be axiomatic that the content of the word God is to be found in what it acually stands for in human experience. It is the growth of this content within

Western civilization that I have attempted to trace in these lectures.

The substance of this volume was given in a series of lectures before the Ohio State University in the spring of 1930. In revising and expanding them it has not seemed advisable to change the general approach or method.

CONTENTS

Present-day interest in God. I. The historical approach to the idea of God; some idea of God implied by metaphysics. II. The origin of religion in the urge of life; the religious idea of God results from religious behavior. III. Ideas of God are dependent upon social mind-sets; origin and nature of patterns; pattern-making process in all thought; social experience included in the patterns expressing the idea of God. IV. The transformation of social behavior into religious patterns; social customs and the idea of God illustrated by the doctrine of transubstantiation; the idea of God as affected by changes in social patterns. V. The study of the growth of any idea of God must be genetic rather than comparative; historical study of patterns of the idea of God must be centered on a specific religion; parallel streams in the development of religious behavior not necessarily related. VI. The idea of God most completely developed in the Christian religion; the Christian religion as a phase of social development; changes in the development of Western society furnished patterns for the Christian idea of God. VII. The study of the growth of the idea of God must be historical rather than critical; patterns to be regarded functionally rather than literally.

CHAPTER II

Difference between primitive society and that of modern times. I. The power of the mysterious; one difference between primitive and modern man is the attitude toward that which is unknown. II. Religion the outcome of the urge of life to come to terms with the mysterious; social experience the only technique available to the primitive man; inclusion of nature in personal patterns. III. The development of religious behavior and social process; religion and magic. IV. Art as an assistance to the formation of personal patterns. V. Tribal gods in tribal religion; as-

ix

pects of personal adjustment to the universe. VI. The identity of religious behavior with social customs seen in the effect of interracial contacts; the effect of Western civilization on primitive society; the persistence of a primitive pattern.

CHAPTER III

Materials at the disposal of the historian of the Christian idea of God. I. Hebrew religion a development from primitive religion, not shaped by philosophy but by social history. II. The appearance of the God Jahweh; the early stages of the Hebrew religion not monotheistic. III. Expansion of the idea of Jahweh because of the change from the nomadic to the agricultural life; Jahweh and the baalim. IV. Effect of the development of the Hebrew nation on the idea of Jahweh; invisibility of Jahweh; the prophets of the eighth century; prophetic monotheism. V. The effect of international crises on the idea of Jahweh; he is regarded as more than a national god; national misfortunes a form of his discipline. VI. Cosmological idea of Jahweh the result of and based upon contemporary science; Jahweh regarded as the creator of the universe. VII. Jahweh as law-giver; his character and will the basis of morals; morals rather than sacrifice to characterize his worship. VIII. Anthropomorphism in the conception of Jahweh; prescientific psychology furnished the conception of his spirit; influence of contemporary polytheism. IX. Reactionary groups in the Hebrew society; the effect of the Dispersion upon later Hebrew thought. X. The rise of legalism as a phase of Hebrew religion. XI. The God of the Jewish apocalypses; his struggle with the kingdom of Satan. XII. Christianity as the outcome of a revolutionary religious psychology; the Jesus of the gospels; his teaching concerned God as Father; the influence of his teaching upon the development of the Christian idea of God less than that of belief as to his person. XIII. The development of the Christian movement under Paul; persistence of the Hebrew idea of God. XIV. The place of Hebrew monotheism in the religion of Western Europe.

CHAPTER IV

Difference between the Semitic and the Aryan religious attitudes. I. Primitive Greek religion of less importance than its later developments. II. Monotheism as organized

in the Eastern and the Western Empire; imperialism creative in the West; the triumph of the imperial pattern of God due to the experience of the Western Empire. II. The beginnings of and attempt at philosophical organization of the idea of God in the West; Augustine; Erigena; the effect of the politics of the Dark Ages upon the idea of God. III. Scholasticism as a phase of the effort to obtain religious unity; Anselm; the effect of feudalism upon the idea of God; the increasing influence of Aristotle upon theology; Thomas Aquinas organizes the theological conception of God; the complementary influence of mysticism. IV. The political aspects of the idea of God at the end of the Middle Ages; the relation of the devil to God; orthodox theism and popular supernaturalism. V. The influence of the new intellectual currents of the Renaissance; beginning of the influence of natural sciences upon the idea of God; two theistic tendencies in Western Europe. VI. The influence of nationalism on the reformers' idea of God; the persistence of trinitarianism; the political pattern that of monarchy rather than that of the empire or feudalism; differences between Lutheranism and Calvinism due in large measure to different social tendencies; the obligation of the divine sovereign to punish; his divine absolutism in his dealings with humanity; English deism a phase of the revolt against absolutism. VII. The rise of bourgeois democracy; democracy did not affect the concept of sovereignty but added economic elements to the pattern. VIII. New corollaries from the concept of sovereignty made by the Unitarians and Universalists; the liberalizing of orthodox theism. IX. The effect of humanitarianism upon the idea of God; the persistence of secondary supernaturalism; the problem of evil; the new tensions set by the rise of science.

CHAPTER VII

The God of metaphysics and the God of the church. I. The political pattern grows inefficient, similarly the prescientific psychological pattern. II. The effect of philosophy upon theological theism in the eighteenth century; the relationship of a Supreme Being; three modern approaches to the idea of God. III. The approach through the study of society; humanism in its two aspects; the humanist's neglect of cosmic activities. IV. Science and the idea of God; the views of Eddington, Morgan, Oliver Lodge and others. V. Philosophical approach to the idea of God; the philosophy of value; monism; the position of Whitehead, Pringle, Pattison, Royce and others. VI. Philosophy evi-

THE GROWTH OF THE IDEA OF GOD

THE GROWTH OF THE IDEA OF GOD

CHAPTER I

SOCIAL PATTERNS AND THE IDEA OF GOD

MANY years ago the Roman philosopher asked, "Do not all the philosophers talk about God?" If he were living to-day, Epictetus would have to ask, "Does not everybody talk about God?" Scientists, journalists, men of letters, novelists, socialists, mathematicians, not to mention philosophers, ministers, and poets, broadcast their views convinced that everybody wants to know what sort of being God is, if, indeed, he is a being. Societies are organized to spread atheism, and communists who have gained possession of the police power fight God as one of the supporters of capitalism. To some honest souls the word God has become such a symbol of irrational beliefs as to make its use in prayer impossible. Yet there are millions of men and women who are helped by a belief in God that would hardly bear critical analysis. To deprive them of their faith would weaken their morals and dampen the courage with which they face life.

I

All this ferment must have meaning. We treat other matters at the vanishing point of thought with detached

1

serenity. There is the ether, for example. Physicists have taught us to believe in an ultimate something within which the vortices or undulations we call atoms come into existence. Now we are told by other scientists that the ether does not exist. One would think that we ought to be disturbed. If we are composed of matter, and matter is composed of atoms, and atoms are vortices or undulations in something which does not exist—what has become of us? But we are not disturbed; even the physicists are calm.

Not so with the discussion about God. Men cannot regard the denial of his existence with scientific detachment. The ether was a remote hypothesis. Even if it does not exist, we still have electrons. But if God does not exist, millions of people, by no means only the unintelligent, would be deprived not only of an ultimate in thought, but of an ever-present help in time of trouble. To them faith in God includes faith in the personal worth of human beings. It means a morality. If we are living in a mechanistic universe logical consistency would compel us to think of individuals as less than personal. If we are cogs of a cosmic machine our relations with each other must be mechanistic, and such terms as right and wrong must either be given radically new meaning or be discarded. Yet even the most determined champion of atheism has not dared to put his philosophy into actual expression. Even though God may be a support of capitalism, the communist calls for loyalty to his party, and embalms the body of its founder as a substitute for the risen Son of God.

It will be hard to convince those who accept the existence of God that the "acids of modernity" have done more than affect the intellectual form of their belief. We no longer believe that fire is caused by phlogiston and that planets move in circles. Yet fire still burns and planets still move. By the same token, are not men still religious? Are not human personality and human society facts that require some better explanation than analogies with machines?

II

There are at least two approaches to the discussion of the idea of God. One is from the side of metaphysics and the other is from the side of religion. Which of the two shall have priority will be determined by the preference of the thinker. If he happens to be metaphysically minded, he will deal with definitions and abstractions. If, however, he is historically minded, he finds his line of thought already made for him. He will study the idea of God as it has been variously organized in that form of social behavior we call religion. Indeed, he will very likely say that any reality for which the word God stands must include that given it by human experience.

Metaphysics, in the nature of the case, must start with an assumed concept of God. It does not undertake to explain how the concept arose, but what the term stands for. Indeed it may be all but undefined. But to argue that God exists is to argue that something behind experience corresponding to an already accepted definition exists. The definition may be exceedingly vague—generic rather than specific, but the metaphysician in discussing the existence of God necessarily, though usually unconsciously, employs terms that have already some sort of meaning. To argue that God must exist is to presuppose some meaning in the word God. The philosopher has had his place in rationalizing religious behavior and the metaphysician has had his influence upon the theologian. But neither originated the idea of God. They inherited it from some social order. They have helped men to see the larger content of their own term, and they have given us world-views in which something akin to human personality is an essential element; but their aid belongs to the stage of rationalization rather than of origin.

Similarly in the case of the word value, definition implies history. If men had not discovered that for which the word value stands, evidently there would be no meaning in the word. Even though that meaning be very general, without definite content, it presupposes some sort of experience which makes it possible to distinguish between the thought of that which has and that which lacks sufficient significance to become an end of action. To use the term "value" in a definition of God is tacitly to assume meanings. Just as when one reaches the frontier of primitivity one finds traces of an experience that is still more primitive, so when we reach the frontier of a definition of words used by philosophy, we find ourselves confronted by still older usage. Nor, when all content vanishes and thought uses only symbols, as in mathematics, do we find ourselves free from the inherited experiences. If we had not discovered that when one object is placed by the side of another object, there are two individuals experienced jointly we should not be likely to say that $a+x$ has meaning. Religion is rooted in an original behavior which antedates all reflective thinking. It is not to be identified with philosophy any more than the growth of crops is to be identified with agronomy. To understand religion we must examine the individual and social behavior of men. Then we shall discover that however undeniable is the presence of intellectual elments in the religious life, men have never been content simply to think about supposedly superhuman realities; they wish to treat them as persons. The social practices of the group to which the worshiper belongs become rites and patterns for doctrines expressing a human urge as basic as hunger or sex.

III

As to the origin of religion as a term representing attitudes and behavior, speculative answers have not been wanting, but most of them fall short of anything like an ultimate statement. To ask why men are religious is a good deal like asking why they are hungry. So far as one can see, the only reply is that they were made that way.

Life possesses what can be called a horror of annihilation. On the one side we have that urge for physical continuity from cell to organism and organism to cell which we call sex. In the single cell amœba its expression consists in the division of itself; in higher forms of life, in the separation of part of itself as the germ of another organism.

This urge of life to maintain the genus is complemented by the urge of each living organism to protect itself and to answer its own needs by setting up a relation with elements in the outer world from which it can derive material and coöperation.

Human progress can be traced to these two aspects of the urge to continuity which belongs to all living organisms, but especially to the urge of the individual organism to depend upon, to get help from, and to coöperate with that environment upon which it is immediately dependent. For all men have what Einstein has called a "sense of cosmic dependence." This urge is constantly expressing itself in two main types of behavior. One of these under-

takes to get help by the establishment of personal relations
with the universe, and the other by impersonal. The latter
form of behavior is represented by the term science, and
the former by the term religion. In its ultimate nature
the behavior represented by the word religion can be
described as a phase of the life process which seeks by
control or coöperation to get help from those elements
of its cosmic environment upon which men feel themselves dependent by setting up social, that is, personal
relations with them. Two indispensable qualities of this
sort of behavior are first, the search for aid from that
which, according to the state of culture, is regarded as a
conditioning environment, and second, the establishment
of personal relations therewith.

Personal relations are social relations. Thus obviously
religious behavior presupposes some form of social life.
The experience gained in society, the ways of setting up
help-gaining relationships with one's fellows and supe-
riors are utilized as patterns for the purpose of setting up
similar relations with the superhuman elements upon
which men feel themselves dependent. For religion is not
passivity but a dynamic relationship. Its patterns function
when they contribute to the establishment of such relationship. They express aspirations and inspire struggles for
ideals as well as for the satisfaction of physical and social
needs. It is within this social process that one discovers
what have actually been the ideas of God. Religious literature and philosophical speculation have their value, but
only as elements in a total social activity. Philosophy has
rationalized but it did not originate the idea of God. That
came from the quest for aid and peace and moral control,
through personal relation with the universe; that is,
religion.

The behavior which constitutes this quest is worth study.

IV

Religious behavior by no means consists merely of group practices, important as they are in social life. Such activity has always some inner conviction. As society does its group thinking there develops a group-psychology. However one may define public opinion or the social mind, it is undeniable that a given group does have an unconscious mind-set. Its various habits involve certain presuppositions, intellectual and otherwise. These mind-sets reflective thought undertakes to justify, but not to initiate. They spring, as it were, out of the social unconscious, finding expression in activities which give rise to formulas which are accepted as axiomatic. The reason for such acceptance may be the supposed intrinsic truth or practical value of some concept, or it may be simply a generalized habit of thought or action which nobody in a given state of culture questions. Thus, for example, we of the United States would not think that the right to have private property, or for a man to defend himself are open questions. They are inherited attitudes of the social order into which we are born.

Social progress is reflected in changes in social minds. A social order, for instance, becomes more complicated economically, its population changes because of immigration; any one of a thousand other forces may cause such readjustments of actual social life as to cause tensions the old mind-sets and social presuppositions no longer relieve. Such periods are commonly called periods of transition, and, if the process of adjustment is opposed, they are very likely to become periods of revolution. Their most significant characteristic is, however, the fact that the total psychological structure of the group is changed. Action often grows tentatively destructive. Confusion as to the relation of social classes will appear in a great variety of forms. In extreme cases anything that belongs to the abandoned social order will be regarded as injurious to the new.

All this historical commonplace has direct bearing on the idea of God. It is the neglect of this fact that vitiates most discussion concerning theism. The term God is not a metaphysical absolute. If human history is capable of interpretation it has varied in its content as man's social experience has varied. It is one of those terms that get their meaning from usage. The most pertinent question regarding it is whether it represents anything more than usage. However defined, is it, like the chimera, a word for an imagined reality to which there is absolutely nothing corresponding, or is it a word which, despite changes in content, really stands for something experienced as an actual element (or elements) in the universe—something which would exist whether it were called God or some other term? It is this question which philosophy attempts to answer.

But why should philosophy be so concerned over the matter? If it does not originate the idea of God but finds it in contemporary use, why not use some other term more satisfactory to itself? Or, if the philosophers so incline, why not abandon altogether the hope of discovering anything except pragmatic reality in the word God? Probably the only answer to such a question is that men do not seem to be able to take such a step. They seek intellectual unity and assurance. The position of the mechanist or humanist in this connection is much the same as if one, not finding anything for which the word democracy as defined in dictionaries actually stands, should say that there is no such fact as democracy. Religious behavior is as much an element of social life as going to the polls is behavior in a democracy which such a critic might say does not exist. Like any word that connotes social behavior, religion has a content, changing according to the particular tension it would relieve. It will vary wholly apart from the question whether it represents anything more than its usage. To trace this changing content is the task of the social historian and the social psychologist. To study religion is the task of the philosopher. But to argue about the existence of God as if there were no history of religion as a form of social behavior is only to increase intellectual confusion.

Social life is more than a background of religion. It furnishes the patterns for religious ideas and teachings. In all forms of thought analogy is the first means of getting intellectual unity. An analogy becomes a pattern when it is so generally used as to become a presupposition of thought and action. The analogy when thus socialized loses its figurative quality. Sometimes the analogy may be extended into a mythology in which the character and interests of the gods are set forth in a scenario drawn from the drama of human life. A mythology is therefore more than fairy tales. It is an attempt to make real the mystery which life faces by discovering within it similarities with that which is taken as a matter of course. But analogies do not always result in a mythology. Human qualities are directly extended to nature, to animals, and to the gods. In such cases the analogy when uncritically employed because of general acceptance becomes a pattern and is treated literally. When this pattern is developed by logical process it is extended into a series of corollaries.

This is as true in the field of physical science as in religion. One has only to study the history of any idea, whether it be in astronomy, with its music of the spheres, or in physics where atoms are described as undulations or vortices that presuppose an ether, to see how true it is that any scientific formula has at its base a customary experience which furnishes the pattern in which new information gains intellectual unity. Strictly speaking, what we call science is a record of the experience and the rationalization of scientists. The exact nature of its ultimates eludes definition. We know how forces act, but when they themselves are described it is in terms which represent experiences with which we are already familiar. Even in mathematics the axioms with which Euclidean geometry starts are really conclusions to which men have discovered no exceptions. We really have nothing but experience to argue that a straight line is the shortest distance between two points, or that two parallel lines infinitely projected will never meet. For who ever traced such lines to infinity to discover what happens there? Even the ray of light which experience has led men to feel was absolutely straight is now being tested to discover whether, with our experience supplemented by new speculations and more sensitive instruments, it may not be found to be curved. Indeed, it would not be incorrect to say that our growing scientific knowledge is born of a widening experience which repeatedly demands new patterns for expression.

In the field of religion such intellectual process is naturally the first step in the rationalization of that vital urge which seeks to get proper adjustment to such elements of the cosmos as are believed to be capable of personal response. The history of religious thought is really the history of patterns derived from social experience by which religious behavior is shown to be rational. Naturally the points of tension in this process vary with changes of culture and reflective thought and the rise of new needs. A pattern, let us say, like the sovereignty of God, varies as the experience of sovereignty in social life varies. The conception of salvation varies as men come to see more clearly the nature of the evils from which they wish to be delivered and more intelligently formulate the needs which demand satisfaction.

This pattern-making process has determined the growth of the idea of God. To trace that idea one must trace the successive social changes, institutions, and accepted ideas which formed patterns. Whatever may be one's belief as to the existence of forces and realities which lie out beyond our experience, the practical reason—to use Kant's term—legitimatizes religious faith by coördinating it with the creative thought-forms and dominant types of behavior of the non-religious social experience. The pattern is functional, the attitude and behavior are the constant elements of a religion. Thoroughly to understand the various conceptions of God, one must recognize these facts. To trace the succession of these patterns by which men sought to realize and use the personality producing and personally responsive elements of the universe is our present task. But such a study must be historically descriptive before it is philosophically critical.

v

The transfer of behavior and ideas to the field of religious patterns is accomplished in a variety of ways but always as a social procedure. Sometimes in the simpler social orders men treat some natural object precisely as they treat each other. As social life becomes more developed such naïve acts are less satisfying to men's minds and are replaced by symbolic acts of the new order. Thus the common meal of the early Christians became the sacrament of the eucharist. As religious practices become burdensome there develops a class of men who are representative of the community and in return for a livelihood may be counted upon to see that the cult is properly maintained. It is natural, therefore, that priests and others who engage in a religious vocation should be held to a more rigorous observance of the acts which bring the god into the social activities of the group, and, because of this intimacy, be regarded as possessing certain powers which the people at large do not possess. They conserve the pattern as something sacred. In social orders where there is no marked change in customs, religious classes like the priests have a very considerable authority and are regarded with respect if not with fear. When, however, the social order changes, the social practices which form the pattern for religion are themselves outmoded and religious behavior consequently no longer reproduces actual customs of social life. As the social changes proceed, the religious practices are less and less representative and become reminders of social conditions and actions of an abandoned past. In consequence, both religion and those who represent it lose in popular esteem. They may be regarded with respect and fear, but such attitudes are decreasingly derived from the sense of the identity of religious with general group behavior. Religious practices, though venerable, are no longer an extension of those which are unquestioned in the life of the group itself. There is probably no religion which could not be used as an illustration of these processes, but the chasm between religious behavior and general social life is most marked in countries where the social transformation is most pronounced. The most striking illustration is Russia, where a religious organization which had failed to respond to social changes and had become identified with the imperial, capitalistic régime is threatened with extinction by those who are reorganizing the state on the basis of communistic theory.

That social customs modify the idea of God and furnish methods by which human life believes it appropriates divine power may be illustrated by the doctrine of the real presence of the Son of God in the eucharist. By "real presence" is meant, it is probably not necessary to add, the actual presence of the substance of the flesh and blood of Jesus in the elements of the sacred meal. It was easy to conceive that men came into saving relationship with their God through this sacramental meal. The early Christians had a common meal in which they had believed the Christ was present. But by the time of Paul this meal had taken over supernatural elements. Just as one might have communion with demons by eating food which had been offered to them, so whoever partook of the common meal of the Christians was dealing with the supernatural. To eat it unworthily was dangerous to the health. By the middle of the second century Justin Martyr could say that the elements of which the Christians partook in their meal were not common bread and wine but the flesh and blood of Jesus. But this was a matter of belief rather than of logic. There doubtless persisted in the minds of the Christians the widespread belief in the practices of the mystery religions that the initiates, either by eating the flesh of a recently killed victim or by some orgiastic act actually partook of the divine life. With the background of such practices it is not difficult to understand why the civil authorities of Rome could believe that the Christians actually partook of human flesh and practiced orgiastic license. But, however misunderstood, this sacramental meal appealed too vigorously to the mass of Christians to be abandoned. The practice of theophagy, that is, the eating of the god, was too easily understood to be abandoned. It had to be rationalized. The means for such an intellectual vindication was found in the metaphysical conception of substance and in the accepted ability of the priest to work miracles. The hypothesis of transubstantiation was in accord with the mind of the Schoolmen, and was given necessary logical statement and subsequently became a central dogma of the Roman Catholic Church. Not only did participation in the meal become an instrument of church discipline, but the conception of God was itself modified so as to permit the miracle of the change of the unseen substance of the elements into the substance of the flesh and blood of Christ, the incarnate Son of God.

It would be hard not to see in this quality of religion something inconsistent with the philosophical conception of God held by the great Schoolmen. But to them there was no inconsistency. Transubstantiation was a fact to be received on the authority of the church under severe penalty. There was thus added to the conception of God a quality not to be established by reason, however much it might be argued that the priest was capable of performing the miracle because of the authority given the church by Christ.

Religious behavior born of social customs has shaped religious thought in all groups. Everywhere social practices have been treated as patterns of thought. Not only

are feasts given in the name of the god, but gods are
conceived of as being like chieftains who enjoy feasts.
When the feast becomes a sacrament these patterns in
which the deity is conceived are unchanged. There grows
up an orthodoxy in which they are authoritative. In polytheistic cultures there is a world of divinities which is a
transcendentalized social order. The gods are not only in
the images of men, but their relations among themselves
and with men are made in the image of social life.

Here again, so long as there is no radical change in the
social order, the two realms naturally supplement each
other and religious thought is a picture of the habits of
actual human society. But when the mind-set of a group
is modified, authoritative orthodoxy is, so to speak, left
suspended in the heavens. Just as the gods represent outgrown social controls, so the patterns of religious thought
no longer represent those of contemporary thinking. New
tensions arise. Religious ideas suffer the same fate as religious practices. They may be respected, but they no longer
represent actual intellectual life. They have to be defended by appeal to an authority which increasingly fails
to represent controlling social experience. Patterns of the
religious thinking which once were identical with those
of group thinking, because of new group practices become
vestigial, unconnected with the creative forces of the new
social conditions. Inevitably, therefore, they fail to min-
ister to intellectual needs and a religion becomes both in
practice and thought a sort of ghost of a previous social
order. The gods act in ways and their representatives
think in patterns which are no longer those of the contemporary social order. Religion inevitably grows ineffective in meeting the needs set by the new social conditions
and operations. The god must be either relegated to the

unintelligent or the pattern in which he is conceived must be changed. For only as a pattern aids in personal adjustment to forces in the cosmos, is it really helpful. Man is no more passive in religion than in any other phase of life.

VI

The development of any idea of God as it has been expressed in behavior patterns, can be best studied as a phase of a single social process. We must pass from the consideration of religion to specific religions, each a technique in which religion as a vital urge expresses itself. Now a technique is distinct and individual. One cannot understand the development of religious ideas by massing data derived from all sorts of social histories. That there is value in the comparative method is undeniable, but the value needs to be carefully stated in order to be actual. One can study but not picture any historical process by massing similar or dissimilar items in independent processes. Such a method may conduce to a philosophy of religion, but it will not necessarily lead to an understanding of an idea of God actually held by some community. As a matter of fact each social order has evolved and preserved its own religious ideas. The similarity between these ideas is due to the fact that certain forms of social behavior have everywhere been found indispensable to human happiness and well-being. But each particular social group has formed its religions from its own experience. Though a group may have for various reasons appropriated and reëxpressed ideas and practices of other groups, one can no more understand a religion by generalizing religions than one can understand the Constitution of the United States by generalizing governments. The only universal statement which is really safe is that at the same levels of civilization different streams of social life, though separate geographically and by origin, tend to develop the same type of social practices and in consequence similar religious concepts. Pre-agricultural civilizations have a behavior calculated to gain one sort of superhuman aid, but agricultural civilizations have other needs. Thus the sun-god of the Vedas became the storm-god of Hinduism. When a society becomes commercial and warlike its religious ideas are set in corresponding patterns. When, like modern civilization, it becomes industrial the question as to what form the idea of God will take is still under discussion. Yet it would be incorrect to regard all religious developments as uniform. We can no longer affirm that all religions have passed from fetichism through animism, polytheism, national henotheism, to metaphysical monotheism.

Two facts seem to be indisputable. First, religious practices and ideals are not always abandoned when the social structure from which they sprang has been outgrown and replaced. Their very age makes them sacred, and in religion a group finds sometimes a holy satisfaction in treating itself as composed of contemporary ancestors. In consequence its ideas of God rise but slowly to the level of its best culture.

The other fact is that those changes of the social order we call modernity involve our religious heritage as truly as the economic and political. One has only to look about to see illustrations of that. The demand, for instance, that churches to-day should be organized on business principles, that women should have the right to preach as well as practice goodness, that children should be educated in the field of religion in as intelligent a fashion as in other matters—all these are, so to speak, nucleus points where the shift in social ideals and social practices, in social structures, and above all, in the habits of social thinking are affecting those aspects of social behavior which we call religion.

The more one studies such processes of change historically rather than theologically, especially in highly feverish moments like revolutions, the more one is convinced that the only way to understand an idea of God is to watch its development in a specific group. In such observation we must center attention not on some alleged theological "essence" but on the behavior and the rationalizing processes of the group itself. For a religion is not some fixed theology or system of truth but action and belief, which constitute a phase of the total group life. It cannot be otherwise understood.

Yet to study the development of the idea of God in continuous rather than parallel streams of civilization is not to disregard the interplay of civilizations. Every civilization is more or less exogamous. Mutual reactions doubtless exist, even though they are hardly traceable. The ancient world was no more static than the modern. The old departmental ethnography that located peoples and civilizations within impenetrable geographical frontiers has long since given way to the conception of history as a process in which human beings are as restless as ants. Looking down upon the ancient centuries, we can see the expansion of the Aryan eastward and westward, the interplay of Assyrian and Egyptian, the commercial traveler from India forcing his way into Asia Minor and Europe, the Buddhist traveling to Persia and Syria, the Persian and Syrian to the Far East, the Macedonian Empire leaving its traces from the Balkans to the Ganges, and the Arabian conquest carrying culture eastward and westward almost to the confines of the known world.

Even though we cannot trace distinctly such contacts, it is impossible to believe that they did not and do not exist. In the Near East the interpenetration of civilizations is genetic and traceable. Augustine's statement that Plato plagiarized from Moses is not so improbable as it sounds. There does not seem to be any language or civilization in Europe or Asia that is impenetrable or unpenetrating.

Yet each civilization has its own character and history. It can be studied as a continuous stream of social development. Its ideals and institutions, wherever they originated, have been so digested as to become elements of a distinct civilization with a consistent religion. The development of the Christian doctrine of the trinity, for example, would have very little except comparative value for a study of the triads of India. There is no discoverable genetic connection between the Confucian and Taoist idea of heaven and the Semitic conception of Jahweh. Each sprang from a different civilization. Functionally they are the same, but in origin and content they are independent. We must study ideas of God distributively, tracing the social origins and the development of each. Such a study will yield similarities, but their sum total would not be any conception held by a group or civilization. In social processes, as in human genealogy, resemblances do not necessarily imply consanguinity. One does not need to be a brother or even a first cousin of a member of another race in order to account for generic human resemblances. One cannot understand humanity simply by massing together the varied characteristics of all human stocks. To insist that one should get an idea of God by the accumulation of details of various religions is a good deal like saying that to have a picture of one's wife one should get a composite photograph of other people's wives. We do not worship a composite God any more than we love a composite photograph. As the civilization, so is the idea of God.

VII

Christianity, historically viewed, is not a fixed quantum of behavior and doctrine modified by social change. It is rather the religion of people who regard themselves as Christians. Their reactions to social conditions, their methods of satisfying the economic, moral, and spiritual needs breed true to themselves, and their Christianity is a phase of their total life expressing loyal trust in Jesus Christ as a Savior. However many truths it urges, it must be viewed as a phase of a genetic social movement rather than as a system of theology.

Christianity originating in a Semitic culture became the religion of the Aryans. Within a century from the death of its founder it had become a religious movement quite distinct from Judaism. It spread westward on both the northern and the southern coasts of the Mediterranean. It spread North among the Slavs, but in neither Greece, the Balkans, nor Russia did it develop appreciably beyond the stage it had reached in the later days of the Eastern Roman Empire. For civilization itself was there all but static. It was among the sea-trading and conquering peoples of Western Europe that social progress and the growth of the idea of God were greatest. The same boundaries marked the birthplace of Western civilization and of Latin Christianity. The same men who produced the one produced the other. The epochs of one were the epochs of the other. Western theology and religious practices differentiated from the Eastern as Western political and economic life differentiated. Where there was political growth there was religious readjustment. Where there was religious freedom there was political expansion. The Western movement of the adherents of Christianity carried the different aspects of this religion to the American hemisphere. American colonies on the North Atlantic were almost exclusively Protestant; those on the Gulf of Mexico and the South Atlantic and in the West were Roman Catholic. The reasons for this difference are not only geographical and economic. Two types of social evolution were there. Because of this fact the political development of the American continents has been affected by and reflected in religious institutions and thought. They all are phases of the same social movement.

Such facts as these make it evident that as a religion Christianity is the outcome of a very complicated social process. To treat it as merely a matter of doctrine, to identify it with the behavior and beliefs of New Testament time or with its creeds, is utterly to misunderstand it. The Christian religion has had its creeds, its confessions, and its theologies. But it has had also its sacraments, liturgies, priests, councils, universities, moralities. Its followers have prayed, gone to the confessional, received absolution, called upon Mary and the saints as well as upon God and Christ. They have attended religious services, partaken of the sacraments, and in greater or less degree undertaken to live in accordance with the Ten Commandments and the Golden Rule. Such acts of religion have been the chief interests of plain Christians. Each of them presupposes some idea of God with a distinct influence upon the followers of Christ. Whether or not they understand the Apostles' and Nicene creeds, men have acted in ways other than they would have acted had they not held these creeds as infallible formulas of the divine will.

The Christian religion as a phase of a social process developed its own characteristic patterns. Some of them resembled those of other religions, but as a religion growing into larger symmetry, and reflecting and developing a social order, Christianity has been distinct from its contemporaries. It passed through many of the stages through which other religions have passed, but unlike them it has neither been checked by nor been able to check the development of society. It is a phase of social order that lost rigidity by sea voyaging and colonization, gained a sense of social structure in feudal hierarchies, imperial unity, and national patriotism; accumulated material capital, refused to hold human beings as capital, substituted the machine for human toil, gained leisure by scientific mastery of nature, and educated boys and girls in the interest of economic efficiency and personal welfare. It is not difficult to understand why the idea of God should vary with this vast variation of human experience and institutions. This fact is all the more remarkable in view of the fact that other religions, like Confucianism, Hinduism, and Buddhism, have tended to hold human progress at the point where the religion itself was efficiently organized. The same is true in large degree of the Christian movement in Greece, the Balkans, and Russia, where social life and religion alike for centuries have been static or changed only by revolution. It has been in Western Christendom that the idea of God has been most freely criticized and modified.

In its theistic ideas Christianity has illustrated a tendency which the comparative study of religions discloses. In all alike, there has been a change from primitive conceptions of the gods to those needed by and more in accord with the new social status. Where an inherited cult and inherited ideas of God have been unadapted to a social order that had become more complicated by virtue of economic, geographic and other changes, the older ideas of deity have either been expanded to meet the new conditions and needs or they have been supplemented by some conception which sprang from the new conditions. All religions illustrate these changes, but as will appear in the course of our discussion, in Christianity they have been carried further because Western civilization has become so much more complicated than that of China, for example. Oriental countries, however, as they have come under the influence of Western civilization, are experiencing the same struggle over religion. There, too, the ideas of divinity are either being expanded or replaced by a philosophy held to be more in accord with modern knowledge.

Such changes are, so to speak, biological rather than mechanical. Older conceptions survive as more or less recognized vestiges in a religion which has become a phase of a new stage of social development. Hinduism has its vast host of gods as well as its ultimate impersonal Brahm; the Chinese have their fear of devils along with the respect for the Way of Heaven; Christianity has its survivals of polytheism and magic as well as its monotheistic trinity. And these illustrations might be indefinitely increased.

It should be evident that in thus centering attention upon the growth of the idea of God in Christianity, we are studying the history of patterns which have resulted from a religious behavior in a more complicated social order than that conditioning other religions. In Christianity, as in no other religion, there has been a unique

development of monotheism. Not even in the cult of its
founder is Christianity more characteristic than in its
development of the idea of one God. The growth of such
a supreme religious conception has been due to no single
set of forces. It is the coefficient of a still continuing social
evolution with ever new social mind-sets.

VIII

Whoever would write the history of any religious concept will always be tempted to sit in judgment upon its
truth. In so far as he yields to this conception is he liable
to distort his interpretations. If we could really know
exactly the relations between successive events and epochs
in human history we should have a true philosophy of
history. But of course such knowledge is beyond us. In
order to understand the present we have, therefore, in
some way or other projected ourselves into the past and so
sought to understand the connotation as well as the content of terms and formulas which we have inherited. The
possibility of misreading the past in such a procedure is
obvious. Especially is this true in the case of the idea of
God. It can be and has been studied by those who were
swayed by considerations quite other than those of the
historian. Instead of endeavoring to discover what God
meant to the people whose social life gave rise to the
patterns in which he was conceived, they have passed
judgment as to their truth, meaning thereby the possibility
of their being coördinated with the historian's own stock
of unquestioned beliefs and patterns. Such a method is
unfortunate. It fails to appreciate the real significance of
a social heritage and tends to draw men away from participation in a religion affected by a developing social
order. Students of the history of religion too frequently

are personally uninterested in a religion. They have become so familiar with outgrown religious practices and ideas that they have no sympathy with the religion of the society in which they live. Having unconsciously identified religion with its earlier stages, they naturally reject it. But this is a good deal like refusing to be an American citizen because one disapproves of the political habits of the Iroquois Indians. What the historian ought to see is that religious activities and thoughts, while relative to the culture and social mind-sets of those who practice them, all have a functional significance. They are attempts to satisfy human needs and as such should be estimated. The fact that religious concepts are patterns rather than scientific formulas enables one to see what the real significance of a religion is. We can discover when patterns emerge, how they help human life to find adjustment with the personally responsive elements of the environment, both human and cosmic, how they help men possessed of faith in God or gods to live hopefully and morally in the midst of social change. By treating patterns as analogies we can discover values and human attitudes upon which we can then pass judgment. In a way one might say that the meaning of a pattern lies in an equation which in the case of a concept of God might run something like this: As a king was related to his subjects, so a God is related to mankind. If we study the relations of a monarch and his subjects in any social order we shall find analogies which have been used to set forth the idea of the relation of the divine and human. The fact that the people who instituted and used the analogy as a pattern were not conscious of it as an analogy but treated it as literal fact does not prevent the historian from discovering its functional nature. Having then discovered just what service the pattern expressed, he can, if he chooses, ask whether what it expressed is true. If he does so conclude, he can and probably will then reëxpress the value thus discovered in some analogy that will coördinate it with those elements of his thought which he regards as real.

Such a method is, of course, not peculiar to religion. It is a type of historical-mindedness which applies to all social heritages. We do not reject all social authority because we have rejected tribal government. We undertake to organize such authority in forms which will be effective in a contemporary social order. Similarly in the case of religion. Patterns change but religious experience continues. We do not need to accept as final a pattern which expresses an idea of God. The real question is whether that which the pattern expresses is something for which we are ready to stand. The issue of such decision is not whether there is a God corresponding to the pictures of his worshipers, but whether it is rational to live in the universe personally rather than mechanistically. A religion is more than its patterns but proper interpretations of patterns enables one to judge the legitimacy of a religious movement. If the verdict is favorable and the religious movement seems to be carrying forward, even though under outgrown patterns, values which are essential for human life, one may become a partner in the movement and trust that in the course of time new patterns may more accurately express the values themselves. It is in this way men may believe in God though He be variously described in a developing religion. For the word God is shown by its history to stand for more than the idea of God.

CHAPTER II

THE IDEA OF GOD IN PRIMITIVE RELIGION

THE idea of God in Western civilization has a long pedigree. Its beginning, like that of all ideas expressing and affecting behavior, was in that stage of human history called by imagination and observation primitivity. Not that anyone has ever studied absolutely primitive society. Even the most rudimentary of social orders now existing has customs and beliefs derived from the distant past. But it certainly is clear that social behavior born of an attitude toward nature taken by groups in which social organization is least complicated is different from that taken by a civilization like our own. Our modern world does not fear nature. If we cannot make the winds our messengers we can make them drive the ships in which our messengers travel. If we cannot control the lightning, we can erect lightning rods and make electricity our chore boy. Not the least element of science is its expression of an unquestioning belief that men can gradually learn to control the forces of nature. Such a scientific attitude, however, is not found among the primitive peoples. They are in the presence of an outer world which they cannot control. By long experience they have learned that certain facts are relative to others, but the processes which connect them are unknown. The seasons follow each other; sowing grain brings harvests; men are born and die, suffer from sickness and accident; the rains descend

and the floods come; day follows night; but these changes
do not give their reasons. No wonder that to primitive
men the whole universe—especially the fertility of plants
and the sex of animals and men—is mysterious. Their
problem is how to gain food and clothes and protection,
from enemies and disease, from these mysterious forces
which buffet them or bless them without any appreciable
reason. To the primitive man everything in the material
universe outside of the simpler customs and experiences
of life is *mana,* mysterious and yet controlling.

I

This sense of mystery and wonder is by no means
peculiar to primitive people. Our scientists tell us that
they stand in the presence of the unknown; and, if they
have the bent of Eddington, the horizon of mystery becomes to them the frontier of religion. Between the
scientist and the unexplained forces of nature there is,
however, an expanding area of fact which has been so
surveyed and resurveyed as at least to become familiar.
Explanations of ultimate reality may escape the scientist,
but his ultimates are growing distant and his attitude is that
of experimentation rather than of fear. Indeed, one might
describe the difference between our modern attitude
toward nature and that of the primitive man as the difference between that which is unknown and that which is
mysterious. The unknown we may expect some time to
be known, at least in the sense that causal relations between its elements may be discovered. In the mysterious,
however, no such intelligible relationship is expected.
Though the ultimate constitution of matter may be unknown to modern men, they have pushed their way
through the atom to the electron and have discovered

enough about what is unseen to organize hypotheses as to what electrons and protons and atoms are. But anything mysterious is more than unknown; it is not susceptible to hypothesis or explanation. It is to be respected if not feared. That is one reason why we have little sense of mystery left in our modern world. If we cannot understand just how the universe came into existence, we can by our instruments project ourselves to the frontier of the known and probe the unknown. But we are sure that the unknown is not mysterious. It is only a matter of time before it too will come within the frontier of the known.

Yet the scientist and the primitive man have one thing in common: each tries to control, use, and get help from that which is unknown but forceful. A sense of mystery is no more a full description of religion than it is of science. In both fields there is the effort toward help-gaining adjustment with cosmic environment.

At this point one cannot help remarking that our sense of the unknown itself is varying. Compare, for example, Herbert Spencer's *First Principles* with any modern treatise on physics. The difference will be at once apparent. Our modern pioneers in the field of science are more concerned with physics than with metaphysics, and what we call the known is, after all, only something which acts in such a way that a large number of observers can combine their thought of it with something about which they have no doubt. Knowledge is hardly more than accustomedness. Given the same conditions we are morally certain that what has happened a thousand times will happen a thousand-and-first time. We push back our ultimate vocabulary to some word that we do not define but use as a symbol to tie up one set of observations with another. The multiplicity of experiments makes it possible for us to make general statements which are accepted as interpretations of what has already been observed. But just what it is that we observe, just why it acts as it does, and whether what we call the law of causality is itself absolutely unbroken, we are not quite so sure as we used to be. But we expect some day to rub out unaccustomedness and so know—that is to say, have no intellectual irritation in bringing newly discovered phenomena into a general conception derived from that which we have come to take as a matter of course.

I trust that these observations will not appear to be tangential. As a matter of fact, I make them, as it were, to give justice to the primitive man. The difference between him and the modern man is due to the origin of primitive man's sense of accustomedness. He had no microscope or test tube or spectroscope, not to mention the more elaborate machines which are to be found in laboratories of scientific research. He had only one set of experiences to which he could appeal—his human relations. He naturally, therefore, thought of the unknown and mysterious as in some way susceptible to the same treatment as obtained within his family and tribe. Instead of the quantum theory he had his neighbor, his superior, and his ancestor. Just as the modern physicist, undertaking to illuminate for laymen the action of material forces, will say that atoms bombard each other or that atoms swallow electrons, the primitive man thought of the outer forces as like human beings. For both the scientist and the primitive man the ultimate formulas are, one might say, mythological, but in the case of the scientist the mythology is analogy and in that of the primitive man it was fact. But to both the ultimate goal is helpful adjustment to forces upon which men are dependent and by which their lives are conditioned.

It was probably from some such attitude as this that a religion emerged. Its origin was not philosophy, but an attempt to get protection and help from that upon which men felt they were dependent in satisfying the concrete, physical needs of life. Such needs were all that primitive men in an unreflecting age could realize. That which was mysterious was powerful, but the pattern in which the conception of power was expressed was not that of the machine, for there were not machines. The experience of dealing with one's fellows served as the pattern for dealing with this mysterious power. Like the rulers of the community it must be persuaded or compelled. And so the patterns of divinity were shaped.

There is considerable discussion among anthropologists as to just what was the original intellectual content of such a religious attitude. On the one side, there are those who insist that primitive man—or, if they are theologically minded, Adam and Eve—had knowledge of the one true God. In the course of time this knowledge was lost, or degenerated into polytheism. On the other side, there are those who would hold that in primitive society inanimate objects were worshiped directly. Still others would find in the honoring and fear of the dead some suggestion of a supernatural power. Grant Allen believes that "corpse-worship is the protoplasm of religion" as folk lore is the protoplasm of mythology and theology. All such opinions are at the best conjectures. The only thing that we know with any degree of certainty is that men and women began to behave in a certain way in order that they might achieve certain ends, and meet certain needs by the aid of natural powers which they did not understand. It is in this behavior rather than in any organized system of philosophy or revelation that we must find the origin of the idea of God.

Naturally this suggests the oft-debated difference between religion and magic. But it is altogether a non-historical process to start with the conception of religion and then undertake to classify acts in accordance with a definition. It is much as if when Adam was showing Eve the various animals in their garden and was telling her the names he had given them, Eve had said, "Why, Adam, did you call this animal a tiger?" and Adam had replied, "Because it looks like a tiger." It is difficult not to feel that many of the attempts to distinguish sharply between religion and magic have much the same philological ancestry. Having made up one's mind *a priori* what religion and magic are, one proceeds to classify various actions of men according to these definitions. The chief difficulty in such a method is that the actions do not classify. To say that magic is anti-social while religion is social is a correct classification of certain classes of actions but not of others. The real difference seems to be in the different types of social experience which have been used as a behavior pattern. Because in ancient days men could obtain their aims by coercing their neighbors, they thought it was similarly possible to coerce the mysterious powers upon which they were dependent for their daily needs. So there grew up actions which undertook to control these powers. Ways in which this was done were numerous, but all had the same purpose. Sometimes it is true that the mysterious powers were used to do others harm. To that extent the practices were anti-social, akin to murder and war. Sometimes they were of the nature of black-mail. Certain persons seem to have got hold of words or acts which held the powers in subjection. If one wishes to apply the word magic to these behaviors, there is no serious objection to using it, but there lies in it no definition, for sometimes this coercing behavior was carried on by an entire group of people rather than by single individuals, and thus one common distinction between magic and religion breaks down. The true distinction seems to be that between the acquisitive methods of gunmen and solicitors for community chests.

The more reputable method of getting help in finding satisfaction for human needs was born of the experience and coöperation with other human beings. The group life was extended to include those mysterious powers, increasingly thought of as members of the tribe. Sometimes they even might be regarded as the original ancestors of the tribe. Figures of animal ancestors or totems might become symbols of a common group loyalty. But here again the evidence would argue that the initiative did not lie in any philosophy, but in the social mind-set of the people. From their social experience, limited though it was, they set up customs which included the unseen powers. Little by little, because of this practice gods began to appear as distinct conceptions in human thought. That is to say, the practice of using social experience to put oneself in help-gaining adjustment with powers which were mysterious and yet powerful resulted in the giving of personal values to these powers. The various social acts in which they were included led to personification. A tribe would hold a feast to which the supernatural person was invited and given a share. Sometimes the tribe would have a dance which was intended not only to symbolize the sort of power which they wished to make friendly, but was intended to please such a power. It was natural, too, since chieftains could be made friendly by gifts, that gifts should be brought to the unseen chieftain and in the course of time these customs or group-behavior became, as it were, systematized under the direction of persons who for some reason were regarded as being particularly competent to make approaches to the deity. Thus from the behavior of the group were shaped not only a religion as organized group practice in the interests of getting help for satisfying needs from supernatural powers, but ideas of the powers themselves. The gods, so to speak, were born of the habit of using the customs of social life to make the mysterious but controlling powers friendly persons. If men approached mysterious powers personally, it was because they expected in turn to be treated personally. Polytheism resulted from such relations with different powers discovered in nature. Each power could be treated personally.

I do not set forth this theory as anything better than a probable conjecture as to the origin of the idea of God, but at any rate it has the advantage of making few assumptions, and does not project later religious views back into the period of origins. It may be at least argued that when one puts oneself at the frontier of such primitivity as exists to-day, group-behavior on the one hand and a sense of need of aid from some mysterious power on the other hand seem to be everywhere present. The word God combines elements which are found in these two facts.

III

From this point of view it is evident that the idea that fear made the gods is incorrect as a final formula. Such an hypothesis is of course susceptible to dramatic exposition, and if only history could be explained by epigrams, it would be easy to understand it. Unfortunately, or rather fortunately, the historical process of which religion is a phase is a very complicated affair and only a literary Procrustes would attempt to reduce it to epigrammatic uniformity. Not fear but the establishment of help-gaining personal adjustment to the elements of a conditioning environment is the real function of a religion.

The extension of social practices into the realm of the mysterious naturally resulted in men's believing that the mystery had been partially dissolved. Certain persons became experts in bringing this to pass. Such men were soothsayers, shamans, and priests. In a certain sense their relations to the rest of the community were not unlike the relation of a professor to the public. They were experts in a field into which the mass of folks could not be expected to enter. But as experts they could invent methods of procedure. As the physicist can produce electric lights, telephones, and radios, which unscientific people can use and so get aid from the unseen electricity without understanding it, so in the course of time every human group developed specialists in the art of getting help from the unseen powers thought of as akin to human persons. It is easy to see why such a class of people should be respected as well as feared. They made it possible for the community to get in touch with the realm of super-human power. If the community was anxious about its crops the medicine-man could tell them what to do to remove the apparent disfavor of the gods. If war threatened, the augurs could forecast the probabilities of victory. If drought or storm threatened the well-being of the community, the priest could be expected to know again how to gain some god's favor. In ordinary times he could be trusted to tell individuals how they could gain support and assistance in the routine of life. Especially were such officials in a position to induce the deities to overlook unintentional violations of the code which established a relationship between them and men.

All this of course involves a development which to a considerable degree is to be found in any primitive society which we can now study. The important thing to notice is that religion is an attempt to understand and to get personal help from that which, though unseen and unknown, is believed to be influential. Contrary to a once common belief, it rather than magic was thus a forerunner of scientific procedure and dealt with many of the same phenomena that our scientific method manipulates. The difference in the two methods obviously is that already pointed out. Before the emergence of the scientific method the control of the forces upon which men had come to feel themselves dependent was an extension of the only techniques men had, and these forces were treated increasingly as responding to personal action on the part of man. As civilization developed, and technical methods grew common, certain of these relations were removed from the area of personal control. Thus the area of religion became narrower. Men could not discern personal response to impersonal attitudes. The old practices might be preserved simply because they were ancient, religious ideas might be still held, but impersonal techniques tended to replace prayers and festivals. The struggle between science and religion had begun.

IV

A desire for reality in areas not yet subject to impersonal control led to representations of these mysterious powers. A picture always helps one to realize an unseen person, and thus idols contributed to the developing divinities. True, natural objects which were believed to possess superhuman powers were preserved as fetishes or as sacred objects, but most if not all religions have gone beyond this. They have not only attributed personal qualities to inanimate nature and extended their social practices to include spirits or the unseen forces in the environment in a personal way, but they have also repre- sented these forces in the form of some living object. While sometimes this image would be that of an animal, all but universally it would be human. That is to say, the religious impulse led to the æsthetic. Worship was aided by art. If one can judge from such primitive objects as are available, it would seem, however, as if the idea of beauty was less influential than the desire to make the object of religion real. Reality was gained by making the god in the image of man. The idol thus became not only a focus of advancing attention, but also tended to per- petuate the conception of divinities as personal. To think of a god as in the form of a man is certainly a more developed aid to personal relations than to think of him in the form of a bull or any other animal. It was a means by which the personalization of the man's adjustment to the outer world was advanced. The fact that the image itself came to be regarded as possessing superhuman powers is not strange. Do we not have the Virgin of Lourdes and St. Anne de Beaupré? It requires a power of reflection which one could hardly demand of the primi- tive man to distinguish between the idol as a symbol and the idol as an operating entity. The really important thing from the point of view of historical development is that the idol took human form and men were aided in treating the mysterious powers as personal. As men found likeness to themselves in their neighbors, they also found such likeness in nature. The behavior in the one sphere furnished patterns for behavior in the other.

V

Another step in this process was taken when the gods were held responsible for protecting the *mores* of the tribe. The primitive man seems to have been too realistic to attribute only goodness to his deities. They were to be propitiated rather than to be trusted. Every tribe, and sometimes, indeed, separate families had their peculiar deities whose care was needed and whose power to requite injuries to his worshipers was indispensable. Within the tribe the gods would be regarded as being observant of the conduct of the members of that particular group which worshiped him. Occasionally, it is true, if students of aboriginal life are to be trusted, the god did appear to be possessed of a kindly disposition, and the customs and institutions of the tribe which he ordained were regarded as an expression of good will. In most religions, however, the anthropopathic tendencies are obvious and the god is regarded as the jealous champion of that particular type of morality which the tribe possessed. Disaster and sickness were the ever imminent punishment for violation of *mores* sanctioned by the gods.

But primitive society reached out still farther. Whether because of the interrelations of different tribes of peoples or because of the inherent desire of mankind to arrive at some sort of unity, it would seem as if back of some polytheisms there was a more or less shadowy supreme god. Especially did this supreme god care for elemental social virtues and punish their violation, particularly in the case of property, human life, and family relations. In some cases the god even cared for the dead. The Great Spirit of the American Indians would be an illustration of this, if there were not some question as to whether the original word of at least some of the tribes is to be interpreted psychologically or as simple mystery. Recent study at any rate seems to emphasize this mystery as seen in natural phenomena like the rising of the sun or the changes of the moon. And in any case it is probable that some elements of the more highly developed sense of the Supreme Being represented by primitivity may have been taken over by a primitive people from some more highly developed civilization. But whatever may be the origin of any particular Supreme Being, the pattern is to be found on the level of personal rather than of impersonal forces.

Thus humanity, even in its simplest days, found it impossible to face its problems and to satisfy its various needs without setting up adjustments with nature on the personal plane. The behavior which such needs demanded consisted in a more or less intelligent extension of social experience to nature. The gods, even a supreme god, appeared as aids in the experimentation which constitutes life. A functioning of the life process for the sake of help-gaining adjustment with elements of the environment was naturally and one might say irresistibly expressed in accordance with men's experience in social relationships. Whether or not this process is now legitimate as a supplement to our more tentative and impersonal treatment of the universe through scientific methods must be left to later discussion. The one important thing to remember is that the organization of the ideas of gods and of a supreme being, in so far as it can be reached by anthropological discussion, lies in the human desire so to act as to utilize personal experience in getting help from those mysterious forces of nature upon which men feel themselves dependent and with which they feel personal relations can be established. Such behavior implies a belief that such personal relations and consequent personal response are possible. Social customs were patterns in which this belief was expressed.

VI

How thoroughly integrated religious behavior is with social practices and how controlling are religious patterns upon the *mores* of primitive society, appears in the effect of contact with a more complicated social order and its more developed ideals. There is no progress either in religious thought or in religious behavior so long as the social order itself remains unchanged. When religions that have resulted from more highly developed social life meet primitivity, as in the case of the coming of Mohammedanism or Christianity to African primitives, there follow the abandonment of tribal *mores* and the modification of various elements in the social life. The conception of God, for example, which an intelligent Christian missionary brings to primitive people is quite inconsistent not only with magical performances, polygamy, and slavery, but with the organization of the family and the tribe. Inconsistencies are not due to the religion itself, but to the elements of a social order which the missionary represents and of which his conception of God is a phase. Where, however, the interpenetration of civilizations does not carry the ideals which are consistent with the new social order, social and physical degeneration result. Wherever it is due to the agency of men who are themselves out of sympathy with the religious idealism of the society from which they come, the introduction of Western efficiency into primitivity brings diseases, industrial brutality, and various vices. Even when such interpenetration is protected from unscrupulous Westerners, the problem of adjusting a primitive society to the ideals of a highly developed society is not without its difficulties. Sudden social change too often results in the loss of many of the older moral sanctions. The old gods and spirits are abandoned but the new religion fails to supply social control.

The history of interracial contacts is in many ways tragic. In nothing is the tragedy more obvious than in the uncompensated destruction of religious ideas and customs which have hitherto been the basis of morality. A primitive people can no more be projected immediately into the intellectual and religious atmosphere which centuries of social development in other lands have produced than they can be suddenly projected into the industrial civilization of the West. However much they may be given the ideas of God which are demanded by the tensions of a highly complicated social order, however sincerely they may turn from practices which are abhorrent to the imported morality, they none the less lack the patterns with which such conceptions are rationalized and made controlling. While they may reject their inherited conceptions of deities and take over the Christian formulas, they lack the intellectual and social experience from which these higher conceptions have emerged. The resulting idea of God may be superior to that of the deities which they have abandoned, but the new religious experience gets only partial content from the inherited social life of the converted tribes. The forces of apperception in the passage from primitive to a more intelligent religious faith are as determinative as in any psychological process. The natural laws which seem to govern the transfer of ideas cannot be evaded by the use of a new vocabulary.

If one studies carefully the idea of God which a primitive tribe may hold after accepting the highly developed theism of Christianity, it will appear that it is not identical with that represented by identical terms among those who make the transfer. It is this fact which sometimes so disappoints the missionary. Primitive customs are constantly reëmerging to condition the newly accepted religious teaching. Yet the explanation is simple. Religious behavior must be consistent with social behavior. Not until the social structure itself becomes capable of furnishing patterns for religious thought capable of assimilating the transferred ideas will these ideas really give unity and content to religious behavior. All missionary operations are a commentary upon this statement. Their permament success is due largely to the development of new social *mores* and institutions which integrate and make functional the transferred thought and ideas of God. Such a process is made more rapid by appropriate educational and scientific technique, but none the less will be a matter of time.

Where social changes are not due to missionary propaganda but to the undirected interpenetration of peoples, the development of primitive worship to one in which the conception of God is more than the conception of mysterious power, and religion is more than a search for the satisfaction of physical needs, is gradual. The appropriation of the gods of other tribes serves to introduce new customs and, vice versa, the appropriation of new customs brings about the multiplication of gods or the expansion of original conceptions of deity. Abundant illustrations of this will be found in such changes as resulted from the conquest of the Dravidian civilization of India by the Aryan tribes of the North. They will be seen also in the changed religions of tribes that form confederations and in consequence are forced to maintain a more elaborate political and economic life. One or both of these changes in social structure lie beneath all of the religions with which we are acquainted. The process itself is sometimes obscure and beyond the purview of more than conjectural history. But a comparative study of religions warrants the general conclusion that the change in religious conceptions and customs, particularly in the ideas of God, follows any increase in the complication of social life. The original urge of life by which men seek to get personal help from those mysterious environing forces upon which they find themselves dependent confronts new tensions and operates within a wider circle of needs. Primitivity becomes civilization. Physical needs still demand satisfaction, but in addition are problems and difficulties resulting from social expansion and more complicated human relations. New gods or an increased sense of power of old gods are uniform results. The polytheism of Greece and India are illustrations of the former of these outcomes; the Hebrew is, if not the unique, the outstanding illustration of the second.

CHAPTER III

THE GOD OF THE HEBREWS

THE historian of the Christian religion has the advantage of possessing documents recording the early development of his faith. Unlike the literary remains of Hellenism, the Hebrew scriptures embody material approximately contemporary with the events described. It is true that in the interest of a more developed morality and religion original materials are preserved in later writings and have been edited and reëdited, but they none the less enable us to trace the growth of a religion far more completely and with less conjecture than in other cases.

I

Back of the development traceable in the Hebrew literature lies primitive religion. The passage from primitive Semitic religions to that of the earliest known period of the Hebrew people cannot, however, be readily traced. Whether or not Abraham is the name of an individual or of a tribe is a matter of dispute, but scholars are inclined to believe that the so-called genealogical tables of Genesis are really attempts at setting forth tribal relations. The evidence goes to show that in the Old Testament we have the record of the development of a single human stock properly located in its ethnological relations by the authors of the literature. A primitive religion prior to that which begins to develop in the stories of the patriarchs is to be seen in the persistence of primitive customs and beliefs and traces of fetishism in the Hebrew religion itself. A comparison of its various taboos, both local and personal, with those of the Arabs and other peoples shows a similarity which cannot be accidental. The Hebrew religion is also at one with that of the early Semitic religions in that it is identified with a tribal loyalty. The scattered tribes of early Semites, not yet developed into an agricultural people, had each its own god and each its own behavior in respect to its god. Feuds between tribes were paralleled by feuds between gods, and loyalty to the tribe meant loyalty to the god. Wars were divinely inspired and directed. To some extent these early Semitic religions were polytheistic, but they could more probably be said to have had tribal gods who were reinforced by djinns, taboos, fetishes, if not totems and fertility cults. Further, the belief that there was a supernatural and magical power associated with certain places, articles, and persons was the property of the Hebrews as truly as of any other tribe. In the earliest Semitic history the head of a tribe or family was the priest. The first step forward in the religious development of the Hebrews seems to have been the conception on the part of their leaders that in the place of a multitude of supernatural powers and beings the tribe really had one god to whom it was responsible and upon whose care it could depend. Its religion consisted in its behavior toward this god. In consequence its conception of its god was developed by its belief in his power to help them meet new needs born of changing social conditions. Such a development was radically different from the practice of other peoples to create new gods for new needs, and for centuries it was opposed by a surrounding polytheism and the survival of ancient Semitic superstitions.

In this fact we see a striking characteristic of the
Hebrew religion. It lacked anything approaching the
philosophical spirit. It seems to take an Aryan to originate
philosophy. Other people have developed religions and
ethics. In the case of the Hebrew religion, we have a
monotheism resulting from the development of a religion
without the assistance of metaphysics. This fact used to
be given a popular explanation. It was said that the
Hebrews had a genius for religion, that they lived in a
desert, and that they invented monotheism. Such gen-
eralization has its value, I suppose, if once it is modified by
the facts that the Hebrews did not live in a desert, that
they did not have a genius for religion, and that they did
not invent monotheism. What we really have in Hebrew
history is a slow development of monotheism due to the
growing exposition of a tribal faith by religious teachers
known as prophets, and the organization of a religious
cult which grew less polytheistic as the nation was centralized around a king in his capital. But that the Hebrew
people as such had an original, monotheistic belief is for-
bidden by the study of the Hebrew religion itself. For
after allowance has been made for the editorial and peda-
gogical elements in the Old Testament literature, one
thing seems apparent. The Hebrew people gave up their
worship of other gods than Jahweh reluctantly. Surrounded
as they were by polytheists, whenever their central authority permitted, they reverted to an original or an imitative
polytheism, sometimes, we might almost say, enthusiasti-
cally. Popular Hebrew religion tended to conform to that
of peoples with whom they were in contact. From the
days when Rachel stole her father's sacred images to the
time when in captivity the defeated Hebrews undertook to
substitute the gods of their victors for their god Jahweh,

the history of the Hebrew people was a struggle between folk polytheism and prophetic henotheism. Indeed, it might somewhat picturesquely be described as the war of Jahweh with the gods of the Semites.

When one stands on the frontier of Hebrew history he finds himself gazing through the opalescent mists of legend into other histories. For there is a justification in the view of Freeman that modern history began when Abraham went out from Ur of the Chaldees. Such a statement should occasion no surprise to anyone who has undertaken to reproduce the ancient world given us by our new knowledge of the history of Egypt, Assyria, Sumeria, the Hittites, and the other peoples whose very bones we are excavating in the Near East. If the late Bishop Ussher, who calculated so accurately that the creation of the world stopped on a Friday in 4004 B.C., has any acquaintance with the work of to-day's anthropologists and archæologists, he must feel the need of revising his conclusions. For in 4004 B.C. humanity had been developing at least for thirty thousand years.

Yet it is difficult to connect the early Hebrew religion directly with the highly developed systems of either Babylonia or Egypt. At any rate, it is clearly not in the line of development of these religions, although in its later stages it seems to have been affected by the religious literature of Babylonia and Assyria. Nor is there any evidence which would connect the Hebrew religion with the monotheistic faith of the reforming Pharaohs. After due allowance has been made for the rewriting of their ancient history by the later and more sophisticated religious teachers, the Hebrews are seen as an offshoot of the desert tribes of Semitic origin, which came into the Palestinian country from the South. Their traditions represent them as having

been slaves in Egypt from which they escaped under their
leader Moses, who had been specially appointed by the
god Jahweh. Jahweh was said to have appeared to Moses
in the wilderness and to have disclosed his name, a very
essential matter, because the knowledge of his name gave
the worshiper a control over his god. Apparently the purpose of the story is either to show that the tribe of
Hebrews had had their own god, whose name they did
not know, or that they took over the god of some other
tribe, perhaps the Kenites.

II

Such ignorance does not argue primitivity, for the
Hebrews were far enough from the beginnings of human
history when they began their independent tribal life. It
would seem more probable that in the reorganization of
the mob of escaped slaves Moses found it necessary to
have a tribal god worshiped by no other people. At all
events, when we get a glimpse of the first independent life
of the Hebrew people they are found in the Sinaitic peninsula worshiping a god of their own. If the Hebrew
people had been content to live in the Sinaitic peninsula,
doubtless they would have continued to believe that
Jahweh lived in the mountains of the peninsula. The
evidences of his presence were the thunder and lightning
of mountain storms, and his remoteness was indicated by
the difficulty of a mountainous region. But the Hebrews
did not remain a nomadic tribe in the Sinaitic peninsula.
In the course of time they worked their way up opposite
Palestine. Their god Jahweh went with them. He had
his tent, his chest for carrying his sacred implements, his
attendants, his exclusiveness, just as any chieftain would
have had his chest, his attendants, and his exclusiveness.

While this chest or "ark" with its sacred contents preserved an older fetishism and was itself held to have supernatural powers, the communication between Moses and Jahweh was usually in some mountain, and he was not represented by an idol. He was a present but an invisible chieftain, the father of his people but not approachable directly by the people themselves. Worship was in the hands of a group of men of a single descent, and the people had no evidence of Jahweh's presence but a tent empty except for its chest and its contents. Into this tent the high priests alone could enter.

The Hebrew people were by no means whole-heartedly devoted to this mysterious unseen god who had left his home in the mountain to travel with them. Hebrew literature gives plenty of evidence of a struggle between the cult of Jahweh and the simpler forms of worship which were characteristic of the Semites. Nor was this conflict limited to any particular sort of folk religion. The later Israelites preserved the memory of a tragedy due to the lapse of their forefathers into phallicism under the influence of Barak and Balaam. They were also tempted to follow the rites of the necromancer and the magician. In the days of the Judges sacred images, perhaps of Jahweh, were not unknown. Their nomadic status made their very existence depend upon their ability to endure successfully the feuds with other tribes. In every crisis they turned to their warrior-god Jahweh, and their victories were credited to his power and his ban was placed upon their conquered enemies. The farther the Hebrew people traveled from Sinai the clearer grew their conception that Jahweh was exclusively their own god. Around his tent their own tents were pitched, and their laws were his commands. These in their earliest form had to do with the acceptance of him as the sole god of the people, the observance of feasts in his honor, and certain ritual observance as to food.

This confidence in their tribal god cannot be properly called monotheism. Jahweh was their god as other gods were the property of other tribes. The reality of these other gods does not seem to have been doubted by the early Hebrews, although they patriotically believed that Jahweh was more powerful than the gods of the other tribes. But by the time that the larger section of the nomadic tribes crossed over the Jordan and entered Palestine for the purpose of conquering its cities, their leaders if not the people had come to feel that they had in Jahweh a god capable of giving them success in their raids and prosperity in their pastoral life. Occasional feasts were established in his honor and sacrifices were offered regularly for the purpose of showing their loyalty. This cult was by no means so highly developed as it later became, and the conception of Jahweh was not universal. He was the divine prince of B'nai Israel, and whatever unity there was among the various tribes of the people centered around loyalty to him.

III

A new conception of Jahweh's power came from the new needs resulting from the change from nomadic to agricultural life. A developing social order gave rise to new needs and new tasks for its god.

The biblical accounts of the conquest of Canaan are obviously composite. They have gathered up not only the unimpassioned annals of the past but its stories and legends as well. And running through all this literature is to be seen the influence of some editor who in the great days of the Hebrew culture reworked the mass of historical material for the purpose of illustrating and vindicating the religious faith in Jahweh that the great prophets of the ninth century preached. Yet in this developed literary production one can discover how the Hebrew people thought of their god before they had themselves thoroughly changed their mode of life and their social order. As nomads unaccustomed to life in farms and cities, they were amazed at the highly developed civilization into which they came in Canaan. We know not a little about the life of the people who lived in the plain of Philistia, and we can understand something of the bewilderment with which the invaders regarded it. They seem to have been able to conquer and frequently massacre the unwalled peoples, but according to the biblical narrative the fall of a city like Jericho could be accounted for only by the miraculous power of Jahweh. His priests with their trumpets were more potent than his people unprovided with machinery for conducting a siege. To Jahweh were dedicated all booty and captives in a wholesale destruction. When the invaders came into the mountain range which constituted the land of real biblical history, Judah with Jahweh's help could drive out the people of the mountains, but in the quaint language of the author of the book of Judges, he could not drive out the people of the valleys because the people of the valleys had chariots of iron. And for several generations the Hebrew people fought a generally unsuccessful war of raids and retaliation along the passes that led from the great plain of Philistia with its cities and commerce into the hill country in which the Hebrew tribes unsafely dwelt. But Jahweh, even in the midst of these disordered years, repeatedly showed himself able to provide victory for his people

under such picturesque leaders as Gideon, Samson, Jeph-
thah, and Deborah. He was not always successful, for at
one time the Philistines actually captured his sacred chest
which an undevout leader had carried into battle. Such
superstitious reverence for sacred objects was represented
by later writers as far from Jahweh's desire, but they re-
late how he maintained his dignity among those enemies
who thought they had conquered him by the power of
their own gods. The presence of the ark caused so much
suffering among the Philistines that they were glad to
send it back to the Hebrews. It is not difficult in this
legend to see evidence of the continued struggle between
the representatives of Jahweh and a surviving fetishism.

But as we can now see, Jahweh had other difficulties
than giving his people victory in their invasion of Canaan.
Like all immigrants, he had to be naturalized. It is
not surprising that in the process he should have acquired
traits which he did not possess before he led his people
through the Jordan into a land flowing with milk and
honey and, what seems particularly to have caught the attention of the Hebrew scouts, abounding in vineyards.
There resulted a conflict between him and the Baalim,
that is to say, the local fertility gods of the country. This
struggle was to have profound influence on the history of
the Hebrew people for it was much more than a theological
controversy. The question as to whether the Hebrew
people could become in any sense unified was to be
answered. Jahweh was not given any permanent home,
although his tent seems finally to have been located in
Bethel, a place hallowed by Hebrew tradition as that in
which Jacob had seen angels of Jahweh passing between
earth and heaven. As the Hebrews settled in their new
land they found that almost every locality had its sacred

spot where local fertility deities were worshiped. The loyalty of the people to Jahweh did not prevent them from a superstitious regard for these ancient deities who seem to have been particularly competent in agriculture. Jahweh had been an efficient desert warrior, but now his people found themselves in a settled habitation and concerned with the raising of crops. New needs required new powers in the deity. The practical-minded Hebrews who at the time had no sacred literature, no highly developed cult, and no central holy place for their national faith, were unwilling to lose the assistance of these local deities whose followers had been either killed or reduced to "hewers of wood and drawers of water." Indeed, the Hebrews always were in danger of conforming with the polytheists by whom they were surrounded. They were thus torn between loyalty to their god who had given them such success in the nomadic stage and a search for help from local fertility gods who had proved so efficient in agriculture. The representatives of Jahweh combated any form of abandonment of Jahweh in the interests of the Baalim, but they did something more. They discovered that Jahweh himself had interest and efficiency in agriculture. That is to say, instead of following contemporary practice by adopting special gods for special practices, they discovered in Jahweh the qualities which the god of an agricultural people should possess if he were to help them face difficulties and satisfy their needs as farmers. This was an extension of the conception of Jahweh into the realm of natural processes. The change is traceable in the development of new feasts as new social behavior found expression in the cult. In addition to animals and feasts of meat Jahweh now was given presents of the first fruits of the field and agricultural festivals were

either created or old festivals, as in the case of the Pass-
over, were expanded by the addition of agricultural elements. By the new social behavior the conception of
Jahweh was enlarged and, so to speak, he became a more
settled deity living in the midst of a people who now had
homes and farms. They looked to their god for help in
these new conditions. For they now believed that his
relation to nature was not only to be found in the phenomena of mountain life and nomadic customs, but in the
orderly processes of sowing and reaping.

IV

The supremacy of Jahweh to the local deities was
greatly advanced by the establishment of the kingdom
under David. This kingdom was very different from the
national states which developed in Europe at the end of
the Middle Ages. Its point of departure was not feudalism, but tribal organization. It was without constitution
or legislative bodies. It was at bottom military, but it
extended the old Semitic attitude of unity through the
possession of the same god. The conquest of the various
tribes and city-states of Palestine gave rise to a new desire
for this unity because of the need of self-defense against
the surrounding unconquered peoples. Its nucleus was the
tribes of Judah and Benjamin, to whom the other tribes
submitted, doubtless because of the military ability of
David's general, Abner. The conquest of Jerusalem, the
one city of Palestine capable of military defense, opened
for the Hebrew people possibilities of development similar
to those of other city-states like Nineveh and Thebes.
Tribal unification, though incomplete, led to a unification
of the religion. A city-state made new demands upon its
god. A political capital argued a religious capital. So

long as no such political unity existed, Jahweh was worshiped in a variety of sacred places and without any
highly organized hierarchy. A centralized state, with a
king and capital and a palace, suggested similar needs for
Jahweh. Jerusalem was to be the home of the god as
well as of the king. Under Solomon the state was sufficiently stable for a centralization of the worship of Jahweh. He, too, had in the capital a home in the temple
where a few sacred articles of his cult were gathered and
where a great altar of burnt sacrifices was erected. But
the temple had within it no statue or image. The ancient
command that his followers were to make no graven
image was obeyed, and the Hebrew nation had still an
invisible God.

Where did Jahweh really live?

Invisibility might argue that he was absent. There still
prevailed the old feeling that Jahweh was a god of the
mountains, and the legends of Elijah represent the prophet
as having traveled to Horeb to meet him. The importance
of these stories is considerable in that they show the persistence of the original conception of the god, notwithstanding that he had his elaborate temple in Jerusalem.
But the invisibility was interpreted also to mean that
Jahweh's real home was in the heavens. There he sat
watching humanity, so high removed above the earth
that, in the picturesque words of the later psalmist, "all
men looked like grasshoppers." His dealings with his
people were increasingly indirect. He himself no longer
was regarded as dwelling in the tents or even in the
Temple. The latter he did indeed visit, but heaven was his
home. Thence he sent his spirit to certain persons, empowering them to act in his behalf. These representatives,
filled with the spirit of Jahweh, were chiefly engaged in a

bitter struggle to hold the loyalty of the Hebrews to their
unseen god, whose Temple with its remote Holy of Holies
suggested invisibility. The struggle with the local fertility
deities continued, and altars were again and again established on the high places by Hebrews who preferred a
concrete polytheism to the worship of an invisible king
who was without image, or, what is possibly the more
remarkable when one recalls the history of Zoroastrianism,
any symbol drawn from nature. This struggle rose and
fell with the character of royalty. The revolt of the ten
tribes to escape the burdens and taxes levied by Solomon
did not introduce a new god, although it did establish a
new center of worship with a sacred image on the northern
frontier. The purpose of this new sanctuary is clearly
political. It would be difficult to maintain the independence of the new kingdom of Israel if its citizens could
worship their god only within the boundaries of the kingdom of Judah at Jerusalem. So the conception of the
one deity was to some extent delocalized. He could be
worshiped in two places instead of one. But there seems
to have been no permanence in the second home of Jahweh. The northern place of worship is not mentioned
after its founding. Jerusalem continued to possess the
central place of Jahweh's earthly residence. Notwithstanding this privilege of the little kingdom of Judah,
Jahweh continued to be the God of Israel, although it is
not clear as to how the worship at the Temple was adjusted to the two kingdoms. But one thing is certain.
Neither kingdom was unqualifiedly committed to the
worship of a single god. Loyalty to Jahweh rose and
fell with political influences. Whatever is true of the
great prophets, to speak of the Hebrew people as monotheists prior to the Return is to read back later philosophy

into calls to exclusive dependence upon Jahweh. For generations even henotheism was disputed. The royal houses of Judah and especially of Israel repeatedly permitted the polytheism of the local sacred shrines or imported from the surrounding nations. Especially in the latter case loyalty to Jahweh became a matter of political importance. In some instances, as that of Ahab and Jezebel, inflamed by royal injustice, it resulted in revolution. Elijah and Elisha revived something of the old mountain quality of Jahweh and supported Jehu in his revolt. The legends which gathered about these prophets contain little that was in advance of miracles, yet even in them there is the dramatic exposition of a new conception of the god more in accord with the developments of the later prophets. For when Elijah, to escape from Jezebel, flees to Mount Horeb on the east of the Jordan, he meets Jahweh not in the fire or the tornado or the earthquake, but in a still, small voice. And he learns there that the duty of the prophet as the representative of Jahweh was to carry forward Jahweh's plans in national politics, including those of Syria.

By the eighth century B.C. Jahweh is set forth by his representatives with quite other characteristics than those represented by Elijah and Elisha. The economic life of the Hebrews had expanded beyond simple agriculture. Economic classes had emerged. There were the rich and the poor. Moreover, the horizon of the Hebrew life was enlarged by national problems. Jahweh was preached as a God not only capable of help in meeting nomadic, agricultural, and national needs, but as the God of a nation facing national tasks.

It is hard to realize that hundreds of years before the earliest philosophers of Greece—in fact in the very year

in which Rome was founded—there should have appeared
in the little nation of the Hebrews a man who could set
forth conceptions of his god in words so noble as to be
used by present-day monotheists. In Amos we have the
prototype of the reformer alive to new social needs,
threatening Jahweh's punishment upon economic injustice
and national faithlessness. Born in the country, he had
the countryman's hostility to the rich of the city. To Amos
Jahweh was the one who "made the seven stars in Orion,
turns the shadow of death into the morning, makes the
day dark with night, calls for the waters of the sea and
pours them upon the face of the earth." And this creator
God hated evil, loved the good, and established justice.
With this conception Amos threatened that unless the
nation repented and bettered its economic and political
ways Jahweh would terribly punish its disloyalty. The
Day of Jahweh was to see the punishment of Israel as well
as Israel's enemies. Sacrifices were impotent to affect
divine displeasure. Only a moral reformation would
suffice. To the prophet, Jahweh was no longer the god
of crops and herds. He was righteousness personified.

This stern god Jahweh of Amos is balanced by the
gracious and forgiving Jahweh of his contemporary Hosea.
To this prophet as to the other moral obliquity even
though it be found in sacred places, cannot be offset by
sacrifices. In Hosea also the conception of Jahweh lifts
itself above the national worship of a sole deity and becomes the worship of a God who has created the world,
directs nature, and sets ethical standards for mankind as
well as for the Hebrew people. Yet nationalism still
limited the care of Jahweh. He was still the god of Israel,
at least in the sense that he particularly cared for Israel
and Judah and was worshiped by no other people. But

Jahweh, though loving, was not indifferent to injustice and the sexual irregularity permitted by contemporary fertility religions. Repentance was more than ritual. He demanded justice and not sacrifices.

Almost contemporaneous with Hosea was the all but unknown prophet Micah, who, like Amos, placed Jahweh on the side of the poor. He, too, in the name of Jahweh, attacked the complacent nationalism which led the people to believe in the permanence of their prosperity and safety notwithstanding the fact that the city of Jerusalem was full of luxury and vice while the peasants were poor and suffering. He saw no possibility of reform, and foretold with burning words the collapse of the two states of Jerusalem and Samaria. Yet he looked forward to a day of restoration when many nations should say:

> Let us go up the mountain of Jahweh,
> To the house of the God of Jacob,
> And he will teach us of his ways,
> And we will walk in his paths.
> For out of Zion was to come forth instruction
> And from Jerusalem the word of Jahweh.

He was to judge between many peoples, fixing the fates of distant strong nations. Agriculture was to replace war. Men would beat their swords into plowshares and their spears into pruning-hooks. Nation would no longer lift up sword against nation, neither should they learn war any more, "for they should sit every man under his vine and fig tree (notice the rural Utopia), and none should make them afraid. For the mouth of Jahweh of hosts hath spoken." The god of war was to become the god of peace.

V

The social order of the Hebrews was not unaffected by world affairs. The need of a greater Jahweh was seen in the tensions arising from international affairs. For the nomadic Hebrews a nomadic god, superior to the gods of the other nomads, set the frontier of their faith. For the agricultural Hebrews the felt need was not only of a god who could help them conquer Canaan, but who could also give them good crops. For the Hebrews who lived in a monarchy, keenly sensitive to the differences between the luxury of the city dweller and the poverty of the peasant, the need was of a god who could maintain justice within the nation itself, and show himself capable of self-defense in the rivalry against gods imported from the surrounding peoples.

But the two Hebrew kingdoms were anything but independent. Living on the highway between the empires of the Tigris and Euphrates on the north and the Nile on the south, they were never able to develop a state which reached any considerable size except during the reign of Solomon. But their insignificance did not make them unimportant. They could easily obstruct the armies of the great powers. International relations became a matter of first importance. Kings both of Judah and of Israel were forced by treaty or subjection to side either with the northern or the southern empire. Which policy to follow and which association to make became matters of the utmost importance. Divine help was needed. Jahweh had to be trusted not only to protect his people from invasion, but to determine the right choice in international alliances. But obviously under such circumstances he must be able to affect not only the affairs of the Hebrews but also those of the nations with which alliances were made. It was the business of great prophets like Isaiah and

Jeremiah to set forth the power of Jahweh in international affairs, pointing out what was the wise policy and urging a king not to make his treaties into mere scraps of paper. International policies would show whether a king was loyal to Jahweh. Unfortunately for the prophets and for the nation the kings did not usually follow the prophetic counsels, and the misfortunes which fell upon the Jewish state were interpreted by the prophets as punishment for the nation's disloyalty to its god. But these political crises contributed something much more important to history than the rise and fall of insignificant kingdoms and the martyrdom of prophets. In the literature which the prophets have left is to be seen an extraordinarily elevated conception of the control of a righteous Jahweh, now regarded as the only true God, over human affairs. The sovereignty pattern of the prophet ceased to be national, and Jahweh became the arbiter of history. The fortunes of nations other than the Hebrew were ordered by him. Egypt was his son and Cyrus the rod of his anger. His temple was to become the house of prayer of all nations.

This expansion of the pattern of kingship to meet new international needs was put to a severe test in the course of events. It must have been difficult for people who were told that no nation could withstand the will of Jahweh to find themselves defeated by nations who worshiped other gods. When, because of mistaken political policy, the little kingdoms of Israel and Judah came under the control of Assyria, and large numbers of their inhabitants were deported to Babylon, there came the supreme test of faith in the Jahweh of the prophets. It was natural for many people to feel that national calamity argued divine inefficiency. How could a defeated god be a world-sovereign? If the people of Jahweh could be conquered, then the gods of the conquerors were evidently his superior.

There began a defection toward idolatry. Bel and Nebo seemed more efficient in international affairs than the unseen Jahweh.

In combating this movement, the later Isaiah became the herald of still more developed conceptions of God in his relationship to the world. In a protest all but unparalleled in literary vigor and beauty he set forth the absurdity of trusting to man-made gods, and, in contrast, the nature of Jahweh as the only true God, the creator of the world, and the protector of his people as long as they had been loyal to him and his messengers. In the fifty-third chapter of Isaiah the prophet reaches the heights of religious trust in that he shows that those who have remained loyal to Jahweh despite the misfortunes of the nation would yet see vicarious meaning in their suffering and be reëstablished as a loyal nation when once Jahweh saw fit to act.

Thus in the course of the thousand years or more of Hebrew history by virtue of the insight and expanding thought of specially gifted men, facing new economic and political needs, the idea of God developed from that of a tribal deity to that of the sole creator of the universe, the director of human history. Faith in him was justified by appeal to nature and history alike. The future as well as the past was in his hands.

One region only seemed to the prophets to be outside his influence, the underworld where the dead lived. And later Jewish thought found him even there.

VI

What was the relation of Jahweh to nature? A cosmology was needed as intercourse with the more highly developed nations of Egypt, Assyria, and Babylonia brought the Hebrew folk under the influence of a culture that had made no inconsiderable progress. Great cities like Nineveh and Babylon had become the homes of science and literature. As accumulated wealth made possible a leisure class, the successive peoples who had populated the valley of the Tigris and the Euphrates produced not only lawgivers and poets but also scientists. Their accomplishments in architecture and art are familiar to all students of antiquity. Their literature is being translated and published. They established a calendar and plotted the heavens with their constellations. They faced the problem of the origin of the world and developed a cosmology which, though expressed in poetical terms, was a symbolical science. Therein they differed from the Hebrew who, however poetical he might be, was never inclined to mythology of the Babylonian type. But with or without appeal to the use of symbols the Assyrian and Babylonian culture as well as the Egyptian was constantly influencing the Hebrew people. It should be remembered that the Hebrew people were not illiterate during the period of national and international expansion. Excavations in Palestine are bringing to light evidence which shows the presence of a developed civilization possessed of literature, laws, and various technical skills. It would be impossible to think that literature such as emerged among the Hebrews in the eighth century B.C. had no pedigree. While we cannot actually trace the process by which the Hebrews appropriated the cultural influences with which they were surrounded, it is noticeable that their teachers were not unaffected by the scientific speculations of their day. Like the Babylonians, they seem to have thought of the universe as originally an abyss of water within which the heavens and the earth appeared under a sort of caisson, the firmament, separating the waters which were above the earth and the stars from those waters which were below the earth. Such a picture of the universe seems impossible to us, but to the speculative mind of the ancient world, unfurnished with the instruments which extend the power of the senses, it seemed a picture of the beginning of things. This scientific belief of the Babylonians is portrayed in poetical form in the Gilgamesh epic with symbols which a major polytheism might suggest—dragons, gods, goddesses, heroes—all united to produce a dramatic scenario which symbolized the creative process. When, however, the Hebrew writers who composed the opening chapters of Genesis undertook to deal with the same matters, they seem to have taken over the current scientific conceptions of their day, but they saw in them the power of Jahweh. To call the first chapter of Genesis a myth is to misuse the term. It is a straightforward account of the organization of the heavens and the earth by the god whom the Hebrews worshiped. There is possibly a slight survival of polytheistic thought in the plural form of the word for the deity, as well as reference to the divine "us," but the *dramatis personæ* of the Gilgamesh epic are absent and the writer finds the ultimate explanation of the heavens and earth and all forms of life in the fact that Jahweh had created them by simply telling them to come into existence. It is a view of cosmic origin which theism of all sorts has constantly reiterated. In a way it explains nothing, for it assumes the existence of a god who can create, but it uses the pattern of human intelligence and action as an explanation of the cosmic forces. And therein the Hebrew idea of God was to have an influence incomparably greater than the mythological symbols of the cosmologies of the Assyrians and Babylonians. The second account in Genesis of the creation of man is more tinged with mythology, but there again one sees the scientific coloring as truly as in the first account. For the drama of Eden is a portrayal of a fact which involves the conception of the creative process, namely, the passage of an animal man, possessed of what the Hebrew identifies with the life of the beasts, to the human man possessed of the power similar to that of God of distinguishing between good and evil. If one does not regard these opening chapters of Genesis as infallible science and sees them as they actually were, an exposition of the universe of contemporary science as the expression of the divine will and goodness, the real purpose of the writer is apparent. The Hebrew conception of God was thus expanded to meet the needs of minds that were no longer concerned with merely physical or even national needs, but were seeking some sort of intelligent understanding of the universe upon which they are dependent. This they found in their God who made a universe that was good and created man the master of all living things, because, like God himself, he was a moral being.

Such a conception evidently is not drawn from a political pattern. It is the development of divinity itself to meet scientific needs. But so far as Jahweh's relation to mankind was concerned, the sovereignty pattern survived. He was the divine creator, but he was still king.

VII

Most religions have drawn the consequences of the political pattern and regarded their gods as lawgivers. The Hebrews, as we shall see, did this elaborately. But Jahweh of the later Hebrews was more than a lawgiver.

He was a supremely moral being—a God who made the heavens and the earth, who controlled the affairs of nations, and who was the father of his people. That conception of his holiness which at the beginning simply recognized the danger of coming into contact with the mysterious powers of sacred objects became gradually transformed. Untouchableness became holiness; isolation became moral perfection. Such a change is not unique in the history of religion, for in many cases at first the image or sacred objects which could not be touched came to be regarded as the embodiment of superhuman virtue. The significant fact is the conception of unapproachable righteousness that was embodied in the character of Jahweh.

The original conception of a god as a supreme tribal chief naturally carried with it the belief that he must be the ultimate example of what tribal virtue should be. That which was regarded as praiseworthy on the part of the chief was regarded as a quality of the god. But in his case they were more absolute and consequently became ideals. In the nature of the case, tribesmen required a chief that was warlike, unswervingly loyal to his followers, quick to punish rebellion or dishonor, implacable in carrying on feuds, but magnanimous to his followers while demanding massacre of his enemies. All of these qualities were attributed in the earlier Hebrew writings to Jahweh by the leaders of a people forced to fight for its very existence. No wonder he was "Jahweh of the armies." A pacifist God would have been of little inspiration for a nation that had to defeat rival clans and destroy the inhabitants of a country it was capturing. Jahweh never lost his military character and his respect for military punishment. He only became less the tribal chieftain and more the imperial conqueror. The primary virtues of the warrior lie at the bottom of all the codes. Disloyalty to Jahweh as God of the nation, failure to pay tithes to his representatives, distrust of his ability to save his people in times of crisis were repeatedly condemned by Jahweh's representatives the prophets. He was a God to be feared.

Many of the directions which Jahweh is represented as having given his people are shocking to our ethical sense. His commands to massacre an entire people, to dedicate captured herds and flocks as sacrifice to him, very properly are condemned by us to whom such acts are more or less camouflaged in the vocabulary of war and patriotism. But it is worth noticing that the virtues of the warrior are not those of the weakling. Around them can be built constructive social customs. In a highly developed state the department of war can have other than military operations. So it was with the portrayal of Jahweh. As the civilization of the Hebrews developed, there was need of divine help for other purposes than fighting. New social problems demanded new ideals. There were economic injustice, marital infelicity, struggle between the city and the country, the rise of social classes, treaties to be kept or denounced, commercial policies, sanitary practices and health regulations—indeed, to a greater or less degree all the problems and difficulties and social tensions that develop when people live together in stable communities and carry on activities which are possible only in times of peace. The virtues demanded by such social living were seen to be involved in the character of Jahweh. He not only was a God jealous as any military chieftain for the recognition of his rights, but he also was keen for establishing justice among his followers. This was the message of the prophets who in the eighth century were

touched by the sufferings of the poor and the exploitation
of the nation by the unscrupulous rich. Jahweh cared for
the poor. Some day he would put down the mighty from
their seats and elevate the lowly. He was an ever-growing
embodiment of the ideals demanded by expanding social
behavior.

Jahweh was sensitive to the maintenance of the family
and chastity among the unmarried. He himself was chaste.
Unlike the gods of the heathen he was above sexual lapses.
Unlike that of polytheism, Hebrew anthropomorphism
included no scandal about its God. He had no consort or
female companions. In days when phallicism was ramp-
ant his holiness was that of the self-controlled rather
than the sensuous nature.

He punished lapses in loyalty of his people—national
calamity was thus explained by the prophets—but he was
also forgiving. When they returned to him like an erring
wife to a husband, he would be as self-sacrificing as
Hosea. Though his people's sins were as scarlet they
would be made white as snow. Some of the most pathetic
appeals ever made to a nation came from prophets to
Israel and Judah. Jahweh asked only loyalty to himself
and justice in social affairs as a condition of national
prosperity.

It was at this point that the conception of Jahweh
passed beyond the conventional ideas that God could be
bought off with sacrifices or made well disposed by the
flattery of worship. In the name of Jahweh prophets like
Jeremiah and Micah repudiated such unworthy conceptions. Jahweh did not need sacrifices. The self-satisfac-
tion of the ritualists who thought that the maintenance
of the Temple and its worship would insure divine bless-
ing was emphatically denied. What Jahweh wanted of his

people was clean hearts and the giving of justice, the avoidance of crime and evil desire.

Thus the growth of the idea of God among the Hebrew people was not a mechanical combination of social practices. In the hands of the great moral teachers anthropomorphism was a growing organization of Hebrew ideals, a dramatization of permanent values. However much the idea of Jahweh was due to the sublimation of current social practices, it was also a censor of such practices and a guide to ethical improvement. It is true that the representatives of such ideals, even though they spoke in the name of Jahweh, were not always, if, indeed, frequently accepted by the people. Popular opinion then as now preferred a religion that did not touch existing privileges. It opposed the ideals which bred discontent with the conditions which made privileges possible. But it was the ideals of the prophets that survived as a heritage for later times. However relative to the social processes the ideas of Jahweh are seen to have been, the conception of him as the only real God, the creator of the universe, the protector and leader of a people, the director of human history, the embodiment of moral ideals was far in advance of contemporary ideals in religion, material from which the later ideas of God developed.

All this conception of the moral character of religion is summed up by Micah in the famous words:

> Wherewith shall I come before Jahweh,
> And bow myself before the high God?
> Shall I come before him with burnt-offerings,
> With calves a year old?
> Will Jahweh be pleased with thousands of lambs,
> Or with ten thousand rivers of oil?
> Shall I give my first-born for my transgression,
> The fruit of my body for the sin of my soul?

He hath shown thee, O man, what is good
And what Jahweh requires of thee—
To act justly, to love mercy, and to walk humbly
  with thy God.

VIII

The growth of this conception of Jahweh was by no
means uniform. The rank and file of the Hebrew people
were incapable of sharing in the religious insight and
intuition of the prophet. Nor is this strange. Their God
was unseen and his existence could be argued only from
their own experiences or those of their fathers. The
prophets might champion the cause of an invisible God
by setting him forth as the maker of heaven and earth,
the one who had led their fathers out from Egypt, and
whose punitive or helpful action accounted for the fortunes of his people. But the man who had no such
prophetic assurance wanted a more tangible God. They
were in fact surrounded by influences which made toward
idolatry. The nations with whom they came in contact
in peace and war had gods that either were or were represented by idols whom they worshiped. Such sacred objects
were treated outright as gods and not as means of realizing
a God who was actually invisible. There is no indication
that all religious leaders of the Hebrew people thought
that these idols were symbols of the true God Jahweh
or that the various gods of the nations were representations of any single deity. On the contrary, they spoke of
Dagon, Moloch, Baal and other gods as if, though inferior, they were just as real as Jahweh. In the early stage
of the conflict between the prophets and the idolaters the
issue seems to have been one of efficiency. Only the later
poets and seers of the Hebrew people could speak of the

idols as mere pieces of stone and stocks of trees, whereas
Jahweh had made the heavens.

The inhibited desire to portray Jahweh for the sake of
making him real found expression in folk story and re-
written history. Whatever may have been their origin,
the Old Testament abounds in accounts of meetings with
Jahweh on the part of persons long since dead. Moses
talked with him face to face, but that being unsafe for
Elijah, the prophet was permitted to see Jahweh's back.
Sometimes this supernatural visitor is called the "angel of
Jahweh" whom theologians were later to identify with
the second person of the trinity. But the Hebrew literature knows of no such metaphysical refinement. The
angel of the Lord ate and wrestled and performed various
miraculous acts. The stories of these theophanies served
to give actuality to the invisible Jahweh and were com-
pensatory for the absence of images of the god. Even
among the prophets Jahweh was described with such vivid
anthropomorphism as to enable persons to form a mental
picture of his appearance. Not only was he portrayed as
an old man with white hair, but he had passions and
policies like those of the rulers of his time; his emotions
and thoughts were described in physiological terms, like
heart and kidneys and bowels, which were applied to
men. Even something of the primitive phase seems to
have survived in poetic thought, for the thunder is described as being his voice.

Current psychology furnished the terms for anthropomorphism, or rather a sort of sublimated physiological
psychology. Not only did the prophets speak of Jahweh's
heart and other organs which were supposed to be the
seat of emotions, but, Jahweh, like men, had a spirit. As
men's spirits could leave them and travel to distant points,

as in dreams, so Jahweh could send his spirit to different people and give them something of the divine efficiency.

The conception of God as spirit did not appear in the Old Testament. To the theologizing historians who in the eighth century unified and expanded the literary data of their religion, God was not a spirit but possessed a spirit. It was this spirit that brooded over chaos at the creation, who gave men new powers for certain tasks, who came upon men and made them prophets. Indeed, until the late Hebrew thinkers became dualists, misfortunes like the insanity of Saul could be attributed to Jahweh either directly or through his sending his spirit. If he were invisible it was not because he was spiritually conceived but because he was spatially absent. However refined its anthropomorphism became, Hebrew religious thought was an extension of current psychology. Even in the case of Paul this is true. In one of his most striking arguments he speaks of the spirit as knowing the things of God just as the spirit of man knows the things of men. Invisibility might imply, under a different psychological pattern, the possibility of God's being an immaterial spirit possessed of reason and will without bodily form, but the Hebrew thought was not sufficiently philosophical to pass beyond its prescientific psychology. Jahweh did not come to men but sent his spirit. The problem of ubiquity was thus answered. Though the worshiper took the wings of the morning and flew to the uttermost extent of the waters, God's right hand was there to support him, though he ascended into heaven he was there, though he went to the abode of the departed spirits, there, too, would he find God. To the philosophical type of mind such expressions immediately suggest a quality of being which is not subject to space and time. But in the mind which is not philosophical but rich in poetical analogy, no such conclusion emerges.

It seems never to have occurred even to the prophets to regard these pictures and descriptions critically as psychological devices for assisting personal adjustment to cosmic activities. Indeed, such a line of thought was altogether foreign to the Hebrews of the biblical times. Not until the Alexandrian period, when great bodies of Jews came under the influence of Greek culture in the cities of the Mediterranean world, did philosophy really become of interest to Jewish religious thinkers. The book of Job is a poetic discussion of the relation of God to human ills, but it reaches no theodicy except the propriety of accepting his will as final and just. Then there grew up a habit of using the wisdom of Jahweh as the personified power through whom he acted. Literature like Proverbs and Ecclesiasticus in which these views are set forth is not metaphysical, but full of a poetical anthropomorphism which was a substitute for contemporary philosophical systems. Indeed there is even a tendency to personify both Wisdom and the Word. Jews like Philo and Josephus were sensitive to the problem involved in biblical anthropomorphism and interpreted scriptural passages in such a way as to deprive them of their naïveté. All such efforts tended to depersonalize the conception of Jahweh found in the sacred literature of their people but seem to have been confined to intellectual circles. As a matter of fact, they were another illustration of the tendency of the Jews to compromise with, if not to appropriate, the religions of non-Jewish peoples. They had little or no effect upon the actual development of the Jewish religion within Palestine itself. Until the destruction of the Temple, the direction of this development was a definite

attempt to regard Jahweh as the only God, to treat him as
an unseen sovereign of the Jewish people, and to insure
his aid by keeping his law, both ritualistic and moral.
With the destruction of the Temple this loyalty to Jahweh
as a means to gaining his assistance for ethnic imperialism
was limited to the latter form of religious behavior. His
dealings with his people were all described in the patterns
of contemporary politics. He made treaties or covenants
with his people in which his action was dependent upon
the faithfulness with which his people met the stipula-
tions of the agreement.

IX

In this connection it should be said that throughout the
history of the developing Hebrew religion prior to the
rabbinical period there were always groups within the
Hebrew society who opposed the course religion was taking. So far from sympathizing with the tendency of the
religious thought and practice to embody new social conditions, they undertook to preserve the religious behavior
which belonged to the nomadic stage. Groups like the
Rechabites, the Nazarites, and, indeed, to some extent
rural prophets like Amos, were opposed to urban development and championed practices and ideals which were
those of the less developed social stage. The growing
complexity of life which led to development in religious
thought and practices seemed evidences of decay. They
would draw the standards of life from the older social
customs. Jahweh was to them the god of Sinai.

That these "wee free" parties among the Hebrews were
not without justification for their fear of the effect of
social change upon religion appears clearly from the effects
of the impact of Hellenism upon the Jewish life and

thought. The facts at our disposal, however, do not warrant us in any detailed description of the process from the conquest of Alexander to the rise of the Maccabean state. Josephus knows little about this period and the use of the Mishna to set forth the religious conceptions of the time is exposed to the danger of reading into the period religious ideals of a later date. It is apparent, however, that the Hebrew state was in eclipse. The migration of the Jews from Palestine into the cities of the Mediterranean was constant, and with them must have gone much of the energy that could find no expression in an impoverished and subject state. Within the Dispersion, especially at Alexandria, there was some interest in Greek culture, and we know the names of a very considerable number of Jewish philosophers belonging to the Alexandrian period. But their works are lost, and we are forced to study the effect of Greek culture upon Jewish thought by the study of the earlier Apocrypha and the elaborate but later work of Philo. So far as the conception of God is concerned, it would seem that the Jewish people, bereft of anything like the older prophetic teaching, tended to make a minute application of the law to human life and at the same time, because of Persian influence, to reinforce the popular religious attitudes by stories of miracles. Angels began to grow prominent as the companions of a God whose name was not to be pronounced. Magicians grew common. We can recognize also something of which contemporary Jews seem to have been unconscious, namely, the struggle between the belief in an invisible and all but omnipresent God with that of a deity whose worship was localized in a single Temple at Jerusalem. The synagogue with its instruction as to the power of Jahweh and the necessity of keeping his law, was building up a theistic conception which made the Temple worship anachronistic, although, as long as there was a Temple at Jerusalem, the older sacrificial practices were regarded as still an essential element of religion. Pilgrimages to Jerusalem were constant and a temple was erected in Heliopolis for the convenience of the Jews in Egypt.

The few sayings of the rabbis which can be historically located in the last two pre-Christian centuries have to do more with moral conduct than with strictly theological matters. The development of the Wisdom literature, however, with its all but personification of the divine Wisdom, clearly shows the effect of the Greek religious thought. But while Wisdom became a sort of intermediary between God and the creative process, it was much more a moral conception. The fear of the Lord was the beginning of Wisdom, and this Wisdom, which cried aloud in the streets, summoned men to noble living. Evidently we have here a movement of thought supplementary to the development of the legalism which sought to find a command of Jahweh for each separate act of life. By it was emphasized an inner attitude of spirit much more in accord with the philosophy of the Greeks than with meticulous observations of statutes given by God. The syncretism which became contagious wherever Hellenistic influences were felt, did not destroy the devotion to the national deity, but served to give it a quasi-philosophical basis. How far such a process could go is to be seen in the voluminous discussions of Philo.

X

The vanishing point of the developed Hebrew monotheism was morality. Jahweh's law was to be obeyed. It was inevitable, therefore, that the pious among the

Hebrew people should increasingly endeavor to extend his will to the details of life. A people who were under the special guidance of the only God of the universe would have been stupid and reckless not to conform to his will so far as it could be known. If, as the prophets said, the national collapse and the miseries of defeat were the result of disloyalty to their God, common sense would argue the desirability of loyalty and obedience. The nation believed it had laws given by Jahweh setting forth his own preferences in the matter of worship and the various economic and social practices which he wished his people to follow. The nation's fatal disloyalty to him had consisted largely in the worship of other gods, and in the violation of laws governing not only the cult but social life. When, therefore, the Hebrew people was permitted to establish itself in its ruined capital and country, a new interest in Jahweh appeared. His law was to be obeyed. There sprang up a new type of religious leader whose business was not so much to stir the people to trust in their God as to tell them how to keep their God's law. And so in the course of time there came to be the elaborate system of legal exposition which was ultimately to result in the Mishna and the Talmud.

The worship of Jahweh was developed into an elaborate legal system organized with almost the precision of a modern case book or treatise on constitutional law. Jahweh as the national God was not expected to save his people until his law was actually obeyed. The good fortune of possessing a code satisfactory to, and indeed given by Jahweh did not altogether meet the situation. The code had to be expounded. Difficult cases which emerged in its application had to be settled by inference or by appeal to precedents. Some of the provisions of the law, like those dealing with the year of Jubilee and the treatment of real property, had to be examined in the light of general principles also given by Jahweh. By such means they were explained away or treated as certain sections of the United States treat the Fourteenth and Fifteenth Amendments to the Constitution. The ideal set every individual was the observance of the minute applications of these laws. Naturally the religion of Judaism reached over into all the details of personal life. Synagogues were established for the popular education of the people in the requirements of the law, and societies and professions emerged devoted to making such applications possible. With the destruction of the Jewish state and the end of the Temple cult these elements of the Hebrew religion became supreme. National subjection was believed to be only temporary. When the law of Jahweh was perfectly kept, he would give his people that triumph which the only God of the universe could give.

XI

From the point of view of its conqueror, as long as a subject people had its national God and cult, it was a possible rebel. If we add to this political apprehension the propagandist zeal of a megalomaniac, the treatment of Judea by Antiochus IV is not difficult to understand. The only nation whose religion approached monotheism was, like its neighbors, to become the worshiper of the Olympian gods. The attempt all but succeeded. The well-to-do and official classes of Jerusalem apparently found no difficulty in acquiring the habits of the Greeks. The Temple was profaned and a sow was sacrificed on the altar of burnt-offerings. Jerusalem, the home of Jahweh, was becoming a Greek city.

But the subserviency of a privileged class who preferred prosperity to religious loyalty was not to prevail. Among the Jewish people there were those who were loyal to their God and to their nation, heir of the promises made to Abraham and David. Persecution only intensified their faith. Unable to express explicitly their hostility to gentile rule and gentile customs, they used the language of symbol and the forms of prophecy. Unknown men adopting this new literary form told how angels either on earth or in heaven had revealed or enabled them to see the future. Writing in the name of men long since dead, like Enoch, they could easily rewrite history as prophecy up to the time in which they lived. In the safety of allegorical figures moving across the pages of the apocalypses like the figures of a *Waldpurgisnacht,* they brought to their fellow countrymen the promise of divine deliverance for the nation. The apocalypses were the code literature of revolution in which God was set forth as determined to deliver his people and set them in the place of their conquerors.

The God of the apocalypses is the supernational God of the Hebrews. The qualities with which the prophets set forth the divine nature and program were focused upon the national distress. But the idea of God was touched by the atmosphere of imperialism in which the writers of the apocalypses lived. The nation which Jahweh was to establish was to be an empire like that of Alexander, and even more like that of Rome. The enemies of the nation were to be terribly punished as enemies of this divine maker of empire. The sense of their own impotence and the success of the enemies of Jahweh's people could be accounted for only by the aid given his and their enemies by supernatural powers. The writers of the apocalypses no longer looked at history as a single epoch: time was divided into two ages, the one the present, in which the supernatural powers of evil and human enemies seem supreme, and the other the glorious age to come, in which the will of God is to be done, the evil powers crushed, and his people to be supreme. Between the two was a period of struggle and suffering in which the deliverance of Israel was to be accomplished and the new empire established.

The man of vision looked behind men and history. He took over from other religions a personified supernatural force of evil; Beelzebub and innumerable devils were sending disease and misery to men. These enemies of his people Jahweh would also conquer and throw them into an abyss of fire, the prototype of the medieval hell.

The God of the apocalypses, by virtue of the human and superhuman enemies who oppressed his people, was therefore conceived of as having more power over the dead than had the Jahweh of the Hebrew prophets. Just when men came to believe that he had such control over the nether world or when the forces of evil themselves were touched by anthropomorphism, we cannot say explicitly, but in a general way it would seem that the new dualism in which God and Satan struggled for control of the world and the after-life, was due to the appropriation by the Jews of the Persian thought which, from the days of Alexander, pervaded the Mediterranean world. A history of the idea of Satan would in many ways resemble the history of the idea of God. In both alike human experience is used to give vigor to a recognition of forces which lie outside the control of man. In the apocalyptic writings God had not yet made the devil his torturer. As the great Opponent Satan himself is to be conquered and tortured. But the significant thing is that in these last centuries before the Christian era religious thought became dualistic and God was engaged in a struggle with supernatural forces in which victory, though sure, was not to be won without effort. The God who had created a good world had seen it fall into the hands of a rebel who rejoiced in causing sorrow and misery and wickedness. He had to fight his way back to control in the future. Such a view of a supreme good God and all but supreme evil Being is the picturesque way of dealing with that problem of evil which philosophers have always been forced to consider. It is not a philosophical but a religious solution which it offers, not a discussion of evil but a drama with personal characters seeking the control of human affairs. The idea of God has never lost this new characteristic. Across the centuries, from the day of the writer of an apocalypse to our own, religion has set forth this struggle between the God of goodness and the Satan of badness. But from the days of the apocalypse men have also believed that in this struggle with superhuman powers God would be the victor.

XII

This expectation of war in heaven and on earth, between Jews and Romans, poor and rich, was the psychology from which the movement under Jesus started. It was no new religion but a phase of Judaism. Its development into an independent religion was not due to Jesus but to the change in its membership from Jews to Gentiles. The idea of God which was to develop as the religion expanded was not dominated by the teaching of Jesus, for men have preferred God the King of Hebraism to God the Father of Jesus.

The history of Christianity is a commentary on the fate of founders of religions. They cannot remain in the rôle which they themselves have chosen. In one way or another they are treated as deities. It seems to be easier to worship an ancient teacher than to obey his teaching. Nor is this to be fully condemned. The teaching of an ancient master must be so general as to require application and adjustment to the changing conditions of successive centuries, but when a master is treated as a divine person, the resulting religion preserves that which was really the dominant element of his message. The founders of great religions dramatize their religion. Their biographies are more influential than their words.

The critical study by which it is hoped to find behind the existing documents a personality is seldom satisfactory. The Jesus behind the gospels does not have the significance of the Jesus in the gospels. The effort of recent days to separate between the gospel about Jesus and the gospel of Jesus is an attempt to unscramble history. The Jesus that the church has elevated is the Jesus of the gospels. It has been the Bible rather than the Jesus of historical criticism that has dominated theology. Even if Jesus had never existed as an actual historical figure—an hypothesis which I would not for a moment grant—the views attributed to him by the evangelists could not be taken out from the record of Christianity. They represent what the Christian movement has believed he taught, and it is the Jesus of the New Testament that has been built into the idea of God held in Western Europe.

Yet although the gospels have been edited and adjusted to the needs of the Christian churches of different sections of the Roman Empire, it is likely that they do represent the essentials of the teaching of Jesus. In all four of the gospels there is to be seen the presence of the messianic *motif* and the reinterpretation of the hopes for that triumph of God which the Jews expected. The Jesus of the gospels shares the current belief in Satan and demon possession. He himself casts out demons and so indicates his messianic power. But he does not think that God is a warrior or that his kingdom will be established by violence. In an age that had not dreamed of democracy Jesus set forth the relations of man and God in the pattern of the family. True, his use of the word Father as a term for God is infrequent outside the gospel of Matthew. He usually uses the term God itself. But the Christian religion has perpetuated this parental analogy.

Although strictly speaking, this conception of God as father was not original with Jesus, he made the pattern individual. Himself unmarried, he looked upon religious experience with the eyes of a son rather than of a parent. Therein he abandoned chauvinistic messianism. In the Apocrypha the Israelites are called God's children, and in the Book of Wisdom God is called the father of the pious and of the righteous. Rabbinical sayings dealing with the extension of the fatherhood of God are few before the second and third centuries. Then the rabbis extended their conception of God beyond the national deity of prophetism to the personal deity of religious experience. But while it is possible to accumulate a number of sayings from the Talmudic literature emphasizing God as the father of individuals, such a view was not central among the contemporaries of Jesus. To them the filial relation of the individual is commonly limited to Jews and his righteousness as shown in the gift of his law is much the more important.

The parental conception of God attributed to Jesus in

the gospels by no means lacks the sterner qualities of Jahweh. To him as to his contemporaries the Day of Judgment loomed in the immediate future. The fate of the nations and of individuals hung in the balance. He, as well as his contemporaries, taught that God treated the world with absolute justice. He foretold a Gehenna for the unrighteous, the unforgiving, and the selfish. To him, as to Deuteronomy, the greatest commandments of the law were to love God and to love one's neighbor. The immediate purpose of his own and his disciples' propaganda was not so much to set forth the character of God as to publish the conditions upon which men might enter his kingdom. It was here that his teaching broke with the dominant emphasis of the messianic thought of his time. For the God of justice and the God of punishment was also a God who forgave those who possessed the forgiving spirit. Entrance into the kingdom was conditioned by men's attitude and conduct. Jesus was thus the friend of the common people and the enemy of privilege. Fraternity rather than religious regularity or even post-mortem states is central in his teaching. In the synoptic gospels he is a man of prayer conscious of the spirit of God because he has the motive and power to serve those in distress. Nothing in his teaching or the portrayal of his practice would identify him with the mystics of his own or later days.

Jesus' approach to the problems of life was a projection of that of the prophets. Like them he raised no question as to the existence of God, but argued directly from nature and parental behavior that God was good. Like the prophets he accused the leaders of his people of disloyalty to their God, and foretold national doom because of this disloyalty. But there was a marked difference between Jesus and the prophets in that he emphasized God's relation to the individual rather than to the nation. Except Ezekiel and Jeremiah, the prophets had little interest in individuals. Their concern was national. The pattern in which they thought was political and Jahweh was essentially a king. With Jesus, however, the sense of the individual's relationship with God suggested the pattern of the family. So the God of nature became a Father who cared for birds and flowers, directed the natural forces for the benefit of mankind, and was eager to forgive any man who was himself forgiving.

The pattern of father when applied to God by Jesus could be more properly described as fatherliness. That is to say, it is a word of attitude rather than of being. And it should be remembered that in the Jewish family as contrasted with that of modern America, the father had authority and the right to punish. There is nothing in the pattern in which Jesus thought of God approaching sentimentality or neglect of the severe morality of the religion of his people.

We find little evidence in this teaching of Jesus that affected the development of the idea of God in Christianity. Father became a metaphysical symbol. The real contribution of Jesus to the idea of God will be found in the church's use of his person rather than his teaching. The explanation of this is that Christianity has not evolved as a philosophy but as a social movement possessing group beliefs, loyalty, and behavior that shaped doctrines at the point of conscious tension. Among the other differences between the religion of our own day and that of the past is that of tensions. Preparation for a Day of Judgment and entrance into an imminent kingdom of God are no motives for the modern mood. We feel more keenly the problem set by the need of those social, political, and economic adjustments with which the immediate followers of Jesus and the early church had no concern. The contrast between the two religious moods can be seen most strikingly in the modern transformation of the catastrophic coming of the kingdom expected by Jesus and the early Christians into a phase of the social process. Such a change is unwarranted exegetically and makes it all the more difficult to appreciate the teaching of Jesus about God. Problems as to immanence or transcendence which theology endeavors to answer were utterly foreign to his interest. God's relations with men and men's relations with God were his chief concern. And the pattern of such relationship, if it were to be normal, was the love of father and son. Unless one became like a little child he could not enter the kingdom God was to introduce. The individual as a developed person rather than a society was his supreme goal. But such a person could develop only in a personal situation in which other men and God were involved.

Jesus nowhere is reported to have said that God is love. That would have been to pass from the realm of actual religion into that of possible philosophy. At least, that is what happened in the days of Bernard of Clairvaux when the question was actively debated as to whether love was of the substance of the deity. It is hardly possible to imagine such a question occurring to Jesus. He started with the theism of his people and emphasized such elements within it as were in accordance with his own religious experience and thought. He found his people distracted by revolutionary fervor, poverty, religious depression. They needed new confidence in their God as one who cared for everyday needs and forgave repentant souls

who were ignorant of the details of his law. Whether
Jesus universalized God's love is a question which would
never arise from a study of the gospels. The figure therein
portrayed distinctly states that the prerogative of the Jew
is to be democratized into a universal privilege. It is true
there are outcroppings of an attitude which is not universal. Jesus at one time hesitated to render a service to
a Canaanitish woman on the ground that she was not a
Jewess, but her quick repartee seems to have helped him
to a new insight into his task. He not only healed the
daughter but later seems to have worked among the non-
Jewish people east of the Sea of Galilee. Jerusalem might
be the city of the great king, but he was like a king who,
when those invited refused to come to his feast, sent his
servants out to bring in the very tramps that his dinner
might be furnished with guests.

In view of these facts it is improbable, if Jesus himself
had not been treated by his followers as more than human,
that his teaching as to God would have been sufficiently
unlike that of other Jewish teachers to have led to the
organization of a separate community. Fatherliness has
never furnished a pattern for theological thought. Sovereignty lends itself much more readily to systematized
exposition. As a simple matter of history, the influence
of Jesus upon the development of the idea of God was
due to the fact that his disciples and later followers regarded his person rather than his teaching as revelatory.
The Christians loved the divine brother because he had
saved them from the wrath of the divine father. The development of the Christian idea of God was to be set not
by philosophy or by teaching, but by the behavior of a
religious group.

The later theologians utilized the New Testament to

support a theology which certainly is not to be found in the Synoptic Gospels. The interest of the architects of Christian orthodoxy was not in morals but in ecclesiastical regularity. The problems they faced were not set by any impulse to reform society but by the desire to regain their bodies after death. But this interest carried them beyond the Jesus of the gospels. He did not undertake to found a new religion. He held the temple in high respect, and cleansed it from those who would make it into a market place. Nor did he undertake to teach a new code of conduct. His religious program was not institutional. He endeavored to get men to have the same moral attitude of love toward their fellows that God had toward his world. If God was fatherly, then men should be brotherly. Love was a practicable thing, although at the start it might involve a surrender of less permanent goods because of the hostility of those who did not believe in God as father. But persecution could not prevail against the divine power of good will. He died rather than distrust the Heavenly Father.

XIII

Almost immediately after the death of Jesus the movement which he inaugurated illustrated the process of group development. Furthermore it ceased to be exclusively Jewish. He himself was believed to have ascended into heaven where he exercised messianic authority and sent God's spirit to his followers. His return was momentarily expected and with his return the messianic judgment and the defeat of Satan and death would be complete. To accept Jesus as the Christ was to be sure of acquittal at the coming Judgment, resurrection from the dead, and eternal happiness in the superworld of heaven. This was the gospel which Paul preached and which he regarded as the power of God unto salvation to those who believed it. It was to prove the scenario, as it were, of later theology. The gospel, however, did not materially affect the conception of God which Paul possessed and preached. He is essentially the God of the prophets, though anthropomorphism has become, one might say, official rather than descriptive. In the New Testament figurative descriptions of the deity are absent. He has, however, the same psychology, and is possessed of a Spirit which, with its knowledge of the things of God, can be given to Christians. He is the Judge of all the world. The failure of the Jews to accept Jesus as the Christ, the conversion of the Gentiles, the delay of Christ's return from heaven until the conversion of the Jews, were all determined by God's will. His actions could not always be understood by men, but as Judge of all the world he could not do wrong.

Paul's conception of God as King and Judge, so clearly an inheritance from his own people, was complemented by a conventionally philosophical theism with which the philosophers of his day could have found no serious objection. In his speech before the Board of Censors of the Areopagus he described the nature of God and his relations to men in terms which were borrowed from Greek poetry. In God men lived and moved and had their being because they were his offspring. One could hardly imagine Isaiah or Jeremiah using such an expression, but there is in it nothing which is contrary to the spirit of the prophetic theism. In his letter to the Romans Paul argues that the gentile world is justly condemned because it failed to recognize the deity manifested in nature and in consequence debased its religious life by the practices of idolatry. He joins his messianic hope with this theism by saying that after the triumph of Christ God would be all in all.

The Christian of the first century was not an inquirer after truth, but a herald of good news. God was neither an unknown nor a problem. It never occurred to them to discuss his existence. Their interest lay in escaping the penalty due to their sins. The good news was that God for Christ's sake had forgiven them. They therefore could live joyously even though they suffered as members of an unlicensed and despised sect. God was their father as well as their king, and no one could lay any charge against God's elect. Those whom he had called would be conformed to the image of his Son, and there was no condemnation for those that were in Christ Jesus. The God who had raised up Christ Jesus from the dead would quicken his followers' mortal bodies by the spirit which he had given them. The God who would save the nation was now a God who saved individuals. No other conception could have satisfied a group without ethnic solidarity.

XIV

Through the centuries the Hebrew God as set forth in the Old and New Testaments has been the God worshiped by Western Europe. He is not, however, the Jahweh of the early Hebrews. Jahweh had become a spirit unlimited by space, not subject to time, morals, giving ideals to high religious souls, the creator of the world, the director of history, the judge of mankind, and yet loving and desirous to forgive—approachable by the humblest penitent, empowering those who trusted him with his own spirit. But this idea of God was only one element of the total conception of God which has developed within the Christian religion. The Christian movement took over into its theism not only Semitic but Aryan elements. As Jahweh of the nomadic Semites developed into the God of the Bible, so the God of the Bible by coming in contact with Hellenistic culture, Roman imperialism, and the social and intellectual crises of Western Europe, grew into the God of Christian theology. The Hebrew monotheism, born of religious faith and practice, was enriched with the philosophical monotheism and the mystery religions of the Roman Empire. But the idea of God is still developing as a new sense of dependence in life's more complicated organization, a new control of natural forces, a new tentativeness in defining ultimate values, and a new quest for the good and beautiful appear. As when long ago, the Jewish group, with Jewish literature, Jewish hopes, a Jewish Messiah, and a Jewish God became a Hellenistic movement with a God described by philosophy and possessed of imperial efficiency, so now a civilization dominated by physical and biological sciences, seeking new control of natural forces, new social and economic justice, is shaping an enlarged and satisfying idea of its God. But the process is by no means without struggle. As Jahweh faced the Baalim, so the Christian God faces science and the machine.

CHAPTER IV

MONOTHEISM IN THE ROMAN EMPIRE

THE development of the idea of God among the Aryan peoples was in contrast with that among the Hebrews. Jahweh emerged from the company of tribal gods as the one God of the universe because the Hebrew prophets believed him to be increasingly capable of giving help in an expanding circle of national needs and crises. But the Hebrew prophets had no interest in metaphysical questions, and the need of proving the existence of Jahweh seems never to have occurred to them. The nearest approach to such an argument is the assembling of evidence of his power. The question of Jahweh's relationship to the universe was simply answered. He had created everything except possibly the water which constituted the ancient chaos and abyss on which his spirit had moved. Such a monotheism could make no compromise with polytheism. One worshiped either Jahweh or some other god. One could not worship both. Jahweh was a jealous god permitting no divided loyalty as he aided his people to face new tasks and satisfy new needs.

Very different was the case of the development of monotheism among the people of the Greco-Roman world prior to the emergence of Christianity. Religious interests find expression in a popular polytheism and a philosophical monotheism. A single temple without an image symbolized Judaism; a pantheon, crowded with statues of gods, yet with a single window looking to heaven, was a symbol of classical paganism.

I

The religious beliefs of the Aryans must have originated somewhere in the upland regions of Asia, from which the masterful stock emigrated, but of them only the philologian and archæologist can speak. So far as one can judge from the roots of words, the religion of the Greeks, the Romans, and other Aryan peoples was, like every other primitive religion, a method of getting proper treatment and help from the forces of nature. In the case of the Hindu faiths, social experience and metaphysical speculation developed a philosophy which has superficial resemblances with Western trinitarianism. But its influence on Western thought is indistinguishable as more than possibly indirect. In the case of the Persian religion there was a tendency to reduce secondary natural forces to the status of genii and demons, while the essential religion came to center around the struggle between light and darkness, with special honor paid the sun. The dualism which resulted was to have influence on the development of the Hebrew religion and through the mystery religion on the Christian idea of God and salvation, but it never contributed important elements directly to the solution of the problems raised by the reflective genius of the Greeks. The Persian religion remains to-day essentially an ethnic faith with Zarathustra himself best known as a tragic mask for Friedrich Nietzsche. For the development of metaphysical elements of the idea of God as found in Western civilization we must turn to the history of the Greco-Roman world.

I do not propose to discuss the pre-historic history of

the Greek religion. Miss Harrison, with something of the afflatus of the high priest, enters behind the veil of institutions and language and returns bringing strange descriptions of ancient *tabu* and sacred animals. On the other hand, to a thoroughgoing classicist anthropological speculation is folly. And to us, who are little concerned with gods who died to be buried in doctor's theses, the issue is not very important. The period which concerns us is much later than those which are the delight of the anthropologist. To trace the development of the Western belief in God, we need to look to the religions of that highly organized civilization to which a little band of Jews brought their monotheism and their Messiah.

II

For centuries before the birth of Christ, the Greek philosopher had faced the problem of finding a God greater and more intellectually acceptable than the gods of the popular faith. Necessity, or Fate, superior though it was even to the gods, was no answer. It does, indeed, play a rôle in the great tragedies of Greece, but Necessity could not be treated as an object of worship. Men seldom if ever offered sacrifices to it. They could only submit to its dictation. It was not religion, but intellectual curiosity, that led the Greek to philosophy. Relatively a late comer in the ancient world, he inherited the scientific findings of Babylonia and Egypt, but they did not stir him to prayer or worship. His gods shared with him the enjoyment of great festivals and athletic contests. They were useful guardians of social conventions and international treaties, but they did not help him to understand the universe which he had begun to study. As men began to reflect they began to question. How did the universe originate?

How did it became what it is? Is there any unity in its operations? Is there anything beyond the reach of the senses to which the world of appearances must conform? Such questions did not lead directly toward worship but toward science and philosophy, yet they profoundly affected religious attitudes and conceptions.

It is not surprising that the search for an understanding of the universe should first have resulted in a naïve materialism. The Hebrews could see the spirit of God brooding on primordial water, but the Greek thought of fire as the ultimate element from which the visible world in some way had come. Such a solution was simple but full of obvious difficulties. And at its best it could not really explain either human personality or the order of nature. Astronomy, with its discovery of the regular movement of the heavenly bodies, demanded some better explanation. Human nature needed to be located in the universe. Commerce, colonies, city-states, literature and art threatened Greece, as they have threatened other social orders, with intellectual sophistication. The Sophists, like modern agnostics, raised questions which demanded far more information than the times permitted. Like all the sophisticated, they thought themselves intellectual when they declared the search for truth to be futile. The aim of intelligence was efficiency. The search for truth was naïve. Education became an attorney for one's own ambition, and morality could be judged only in terms of profit. If the intelligent Greek, freed from the fear of the Olympian gods, found himself in a universe where nothing was certain and morals were being eaten through by the acids of Greek modernity, it is easy to see why the idea of God was in eclipse.

But sophistication is never the end of thought. The

smarter the question, the more sincere will be the answer. That answer came in the fourth century as in the twentieth, from the study of human personality. Socrates, adopting the method of the Sophist, bade him examine himself and discover in the processes of thought that which was more general and final than the thinker. Only as men came to know themselves were they really wise. But in thus knowing themselves, men discovered that there were laws which were quite other than those of matter. The true, the beautiful, and the good were, after all, more final than confused intellectual casuistry. But such faith could not exist unless there was existing in the universe a Reason and a Purpose quite other than that of men. There was therefore a realm of existence superior to and controlling that of the senses. Within it the motive forces, though absolute, were personal. With its Ruler men could have communion, and Socrates himself believed that he was under the guidance of a supernatural being very much as the Hebrew prophet thought himself possessed of the spirit of God. Casual as was much of his teaching, better calculated to puncture the sophistication of his opponents than to construct a system of philosophy, Socrates did lay the foundation for a belief in God that was to be influential in Western civilization. He was careful not to deny the existence of the Olympian gods, but above them, if not in them, he saw a superior Being, rational and purposeful, the source of justice and beauty. Yet in a way there were grounds for the charge which led to his martyrdom. Technically it was false, for he did not deny the gods, but in effect it was true, for the ultimate divinity he set forth would inevitably put an end to the worship of all lesser gods, or at least reduce such worship to mere conventionality. On his deathbed, as he felt the effect of the poison creeping over him, he asked his friends to remember to sacrifice to Æsculapius, but Socrates' real faith lay in his supreme conviction that death could not end all because there were in the universe ultimate reason, justice, and beauty, which implied a supreme person responsive to the human personality. Such a deity was active, guiding his followers and granting them power and serenity which otherwise would not be theirs.

III

The God with whom Socrates felt he was in communion was given philosophical status by Plato. To him our Western world owes that dualism which no *coup d'état* of common sense has been able to destroy. From him the temporary and the absolute, the instinctive and the reflective, the real and the ideal were so many contrasts leading to the perception of a God who was above the world— an all-pure Being, immutable and self-contained. Men lived in the presence of two worlds, one of sense and one of eternal ideas thought by this God. To these ideas all the material world, with humanity within it, imperfectly corresponded. In their search for participation in this world of ideas men would pass from the world of appearance. Naturally, only the philosopher could expect such supreme experience, for he alone sought truth, and to find truth was to be lifted from the plane of mere existence to that of personality. Thus God was approachable only by abandoning the material world and searching for the truth which was expressed in conformity to these divine and absolute ideals. Plato, however, apparently did not expect that the rank and file of mankind would pass beyond conventional polytheism. He would concede that the various gods of mythology might be aspects of the ultimate God, but he frankly said that "God the father and creater of the universe is difficult to find and when found impossible to impart to all." The philosopher might, indeed, worship him, but philosophy—even Platonism—is not the same as religion. The fellowship which man could have with Plato's God was a rare experience. Yet he was just and beneficent, the basis of the moral order, and he fixed rewards and punishments in this world and the next. Indeed, Plato so far used the pattern of politics as to think of God's relation with the universe as that of a vast state. But there never was a Platonic community of the pious; and prayer, which is the very center of the religious behavior, was all but ignored by him.

Due to the influence of Plato, God was thought of as transcendent, immutable, the author of ultimate ideas toward which all nature moves. Such teaching was to live. Plato has ever been the outstanding champion of a double world of sense and idea, and of a transcendent God who created the world, but between whom and his creation was the world of his dynamic ideas. One similarity between such a general world-view and that of anthropomorphic theism of the Hebrews is sufficiently clear. For the God of the Hebrews, no metaphysical absolute but personally approachable, was not immanent in nature. In Hebraism and Platonism alike, there must always be the contrast between the natural and the supernatural. In Hebraism the supernatural broke through into the natural in miracles. In Platonism men broke through the natural into the supernatural by truth.

IV

Over against this philosophical idealism of Plato stood the scientific realism of his pupil Aristotle. For Aristotle denied the two-world dualism of Plato. Not matter and ideas, but matter and form stood over against each other. Instead of approaching the world from the unexperienced ideas of an absolute God, Aristotle proceeded from the world of sense to whatever outcome logic might lead him. One might at first say his view approached monism. Form he held to be an active force constantly seizing on new matter in the unbroken process of evolution. The universe is thus a universe of ends. That toward which all changes move is a perfect whole, more efficient because more coördinated. Morality has for its end the formation of a perfect social whole and of an individual coördinating in himself that which is strictly human. In such perfect wholes lies happiness. With such anticipation of emergent evolution, it is not strange that Aristotle found in nature a reason that sufficed for men's needs. Thus his religious world-view became dualistic. God was the source of this reason as well as the eternal motion of the universe. But Aristotle did not see that God had much concern with men. Like Confucius, he would not deny the existence of spiritual beings, but he would have little to do with them. Nature, with its rationality and drive toward coördination is enough for men. Science would show them how to live rationally in a world of reason.

The significance of Aristotle, therefore, for the growth of the idea of God, was in this substitution of reason for aspirations; scientific method for spiritual adventure. Platonism and Aristotelianism, however, though at first sight religiously antagonistic, as it turned out, were theologically complementary to each other. For men have at the same time believed in a spiritual order beyond that of sense, and have looked upon nature as expressing immanent law and purpose to which men must conform. Both philosophies united in giving men the concept of substance, that is to say, a generic form of being that exclusively possesses qualities which could not be changed without changing the thing itself. Over against divine substance was human substance and all those other substances for which there were generic names.

God was thus essentially a metaphysical term, the ultimate of the philosopher. Others had their gods.

After Aristotle the Greek mind found itself in a new world. Visions of empire dwarfed the prospects of independent city-states, and the Greek mind became more systematic than creative. At the same time, it faced new ethical problems beyond those which Plato and Aristotle had organized and to which they had given answers too profound to appeal to the ordinary mind. A newly unifying world outgrew old ideals. Epicurean and Stoic alike centered their attention upon the practical aspects of life. Human conduct became their main interest. The one found good in happiness, the other in rational living in accordance with cosmic reason. The two opposing movements must not be judged from the misinterpretations of their less intelligent followers, but the issue which they raised involved the very basis of human life. The Epicurean at his best was not a sensualist but a humanist to whom gods were outgrown superstitions, and man's desires the standard of satisfactions. The Stoic saw a cosmos instinct with the seminal reason of a supreme being. This being was difficult to reach, but he could be seen in his word, Logos, which stood related to him as speech to a man, dynamic reason discoverable in every aspect of nature and in man himself. With this Logos men should live in harmony. With the polytheistic trend of the time it was not difficult to treat this Logos as a person infinitely extended in space, as well as divisible into various Logoi to be found in different substances where motion could be discovered. In fact, it was the nearest approach to the idea of a cosmic God as distinct from Principle or Absolute that the Greek world reached.

By the time of the Roman Empire the philosopher was no longer strictly a follower of Plato or Aristotle or the Stoa. The centuries had seen the elements of these older systems gradually combine into a synthetic philosophy with the Logos as its center. He occupied a position somewhere between the God of the Bible and the metaphysical God of the older Greek philosophy. On the one hand the Logos could be used by a Jewish thinker like Philo to interpret the religious monotheism of Judaism. On the other hand, whether or not the term Logos itself was used by them, the philosophers of the early Empire found reason and purpose in the universe which could serve as a basis of morality without appeal to commandments or mythologies.

v

The sense of religious unity was not the result of philosophy alone. Social evolution itself was giving birth to a very human god who brought about peace and enforced political unity, the Roman Emperor.

To appreciate the rise of emperor worship we must share in the wonder of the early centuries of our epoch. War had been practically abolished in the Roman Empire except with the barbarians on the frontier and among relatively small forces of professional soldiers who protected the Emperor and served as a police force in various parts of the Empire. Communication was as complete as possible in an age that knew nothing of steam or electricity, and the expansion of commerce led to the establish-

ment of financial institutions. Foreign trade with the Far
East was considerably developed, and became a channel
for the inflow of Oriental religious and cultural elements.
Education was widespread; literature and art had reached
a perfection of form which has survived as a parent as
well as a model for that of later centuries. Polite life was
highly developed, although it often served as a veneer for
a brutality which sometimes broke forth even among the
higher circles of society. Cities with great public buildings
appeared in all parts of the Empire, and law was supreme.

Most important and creative, however, of all the forces
was the sense of unity which an empire made possible.
The forces of disintegration and of rival nationalisms had
been checked, and the peace which Rome enforced over a
hundred and twenty millions of people dwelling in a
territory that stretched from the Atlantic to the Arabian
desert and the Danube to the falls of the Nile, was for
hundreds of years a condition which modern life has
never been able to duplicate. Indeed, it probably would
be true that at no other period in human history has the
idea of unity been more dominant.

Such social unification inevitably found expression in
religion. Peace through conquest had been replaced by
peace through administration. By superimposing its administrative unity over ancient customs, institutions, and
laws, Rome brought new prosperity to the nations it had
conquered. What could be more natural than that men
should regard the forces that made this amazing social
unity possible as superhuman? They were humanists before the humanists. Social and political unity were otherwise inexplicable to those who enjoyed its blessings. As
the Egyptians long before had called their kings divine,
as the conquered peoples had deified Alexander, and the

Romans had worshiped the genius of the Republic, so men worshiped the Empire. But they, like their predecessors, were not content to worship an abstract social conception; the unity of the Empire was embodied in the emperor. He was the Empire's God.

It is easy to consider emperor-worship as only an aspect of polytheism, for it would be difficult for monotheists like the Jews to regard the human being as in any sense divine. For such persons the burning of incense before the statue of the emperor would be nothing less than abandonment of their monotheistic faith. But from the point of view of social psychology, it is unfair to think of the emperor as simply idolatrous. True, citizens of the Empire could look upon the ritual of emperor-worship as the expression of a political loyalty to the government and the state. In our modern times a somewhat similar situation is to be seen among the intelligentsia of Japan, where the significance of the emperor as a center of imperial unity is expressed in certain rituals which in earlier days may have been religious but now are more of the nature of our salutation to the flag. Augustus did not favor the worship of a living ruler. He would wait till death removed him to the heavens. But he did favor the worship of the goddess Rome. For in the Roman Empire religion was a unifying aspect of patriotism. The emperor was an embodiment, one might say the idol, of the pervasive power of unity which maintained peace and punished wrongdoing. Such power, men felt, had within it something divine.

VI

Yet the polytheism of the Aryans continued throughout the Empire in popular religion. First citizens, like

Pliny, believed it a patriotic as well as a religious duty to restore the ancient temples and maintain the ancient cults of the Olympian gods. Indeed, polytheism in the early centuries of Christianity experienced something of a revival. But the worship of the inherited deities was not regarded as an element of morality. In fact, the gods and goddesses of Greece and Rome set young people bad examples. The real attitude toward them was a survival of the behavior organized before any sense of great social unity had emerged. They were worshiped in a mood of conventional piety as a means of forestalling their displeasure. The same apprehension is to be seen in lands where Christian monotheism is recognized but where men rely upon saints to give good fortune and prevent evil fortune.

Men in the first and second centuries were less interested in speculation about God than in life in conformity with him, or, as some preferred to say, with nature. Some thinkers, like Seneca and Marcus Aurelius, were in the very midst of imperial affairs. Others, like Epictetus, were lecturers or scholars. But they were all moralists. Confronted by the religious skepticism of scientifically minded men like Lucretius and the distorted Epicureanism by which the pursuit of pleasure was given specious justification, these men were desperately in earnest. They made the Stoic and the Cynic philosophies the basis of moral appeals difficult to equal except in the Hebrew prophets. They turned men's attention from the outer world of sense to the inner world of their own souls. To these teachers God was not abstract, but very real, to whom, "as to him that administers the whole the wise and good man submits his own mind as good citizens do to the law of the state." Every man might call himself the Son of

God, said Epictetus, who assumed rather than proved the existence of God. The nearest approach he made to a discussion of the being of God sounds more like that of a modern preacher than a modern philosopher. "God is beneficial. But the good also is beneficial. It is consistent, then, that where the nature of God is, there also the nature of the good should be. What, then, is the nature of God? Flesh? Certainly not. An estate in land? By no means. Fame? No. Is he intelligence, knowledge, right reason? Yes." Epictetus goes on then to show that in man's own life there is the knowledge of God because men are rational and superior to the beasts. God is the father of man and therefore man has value. He bids men "to look up to God and say, 'Deal with me for the future as thou wilt. I am of the same mind as thou art. I am thine, I refuse nothing that pleases thee. Lead me where thou wilt.' " And in one of his noblest outbreaks, in which he pours contempt on one of his students who wishes to go home to his mother and to comforts, Epictetus cries, "I wish to be found practicing nothing else than mine own will, that I may be able to say to God, 'Have I in any respect transgressed thy command? Have I in any respect wrongly used powers which thou gavest me? Have I misused my perceptions or my preconceptions? Have I ever found fault with thy administration? . . . Is it now thy will that I should depart from the assembly of men? I depart. I give thee all thanks that thou hast allowed me to join in this thy assemblage of men and to see thy works and to comprehend this thy administration!' "

To some extent the Olympian gods were adjusted to the growing sense of unity by the simple device of regarding Zeus as the name for the supreme universal god—that is to say, enlarging the conception of his powers as the prophets had developed the conception of Jahweh. This was the effort of Plato and other of the finer minds of Greece. In Rome there was a tendency to identify Jupiter with a universal nature god. But the effort was not successful. The Olympian gods were, it is true, superior to the old rites of earlier people which they replaced as well as to primitive superstitions like the worship of the dead. But mythology had too vividly colored the character of the Olympian gods for them to become the standards of morals like Jahweh. The habits of the Olympians were far enough from either moral or intellectual ideals. Furthermore, the worship of the various Olympian gods was so localized as to hinder a development such as marked the early stages of the Hebrew religion. The fact that Greek history never attained any genuine political unity but was marked by a large number of small city-states engaged in repeated wars also ministered against the elevation of Zeus or any other of the Olympian gods into a supreme deity. Indeed, although the comparison would be misleading in almost every other particular, as a form of practical religion the supremacy of Zeus, except in the vocabularies of philosophers, never passed beyond the position acquired by Jahweh before the days of the great prophets.

The hymn of Cleanthes marks the highest reach of this religious sublimation of Zeus.

Most glorious of immortals, many named, powerful over all,
Zeus, thou author of all nature, guiding all with law,
Hail to thee. Thee 'tis right all mortals should address,
For from thee men derive their race, they who alone
Of all things mortal, living, creeping on the ground,
Have gifts of speech. So will I hymn thee, and thy power
    forever sing.

For thee this entire cosmos, circling earth around,
Obeys where'er thou leadest, and 'tis gladly ruled by thee.
Such servant hast thou in thy hands invincible,
The two-edged thunderbolt, ever living flame.
For by its strokes are all things in nature wrought;
With it thou dost direct the common law, which throughout
    all
Forever moves, with every gleam commingled, great and
    small.
'Tis this hath made thee supreme king o'er all;
For naught e'er comes to pass on earth apart from thee, O
    God,
Nor in the sacred pole of ether above nor in the deep,
Save all the sin men do with folly cursed.

But Greek piety was unlike that of the Hebrews in
one very important effect. It permitted the use of idols.
Where the Hebrew prophet appealed to the Hebrew
imagination to realize the actual existence of the unseen
Jahweh, the more scientifically minded Greek philosopher
could see that idols were simply aids to the religious faith
of intelligent worshipers. Those who in later days justified the use of images and pictures in the worship of the
unseen God combined philosophical monotheism with
popular polytheism. As good an illustration as any of this
is that quoted by Gilbert Murray from Maximus of Tyre:

God himself, the father and fashioner of all that
is, older than the Sun, or the Sky, greater than time
and eternity and all the flow of being, is unname-
able by any lawgiver, unutterable by any voice, not
to be seen by any eye. But we, being unable to ap-
prehend His essence, use the help of sounds and
names and pictures, of beaten gold and ivory and
silver, of plants and rivers, mountain-peaks and tor-
rents, yearning for the knowledge of Him, and in

our weakness naming all that is beautiful in this world after His nature—just as happens to earthly lovers. To them the most beautiful sight will be the actual lineaments of the beloved, but for remembrance' sake they will be happy in the sight of a lyre, a little spear, a chair, perhaps, or a running-ground, or anything in the world that wakens the memory of the beloved. Why should I further examine and pass judgment about Images? Let men know what is divine, let them know: that is all. If a Greek is stirred to the remembrance of God by the art of Pheidias, an Egyptian by paying worship to animals, another man by a river, another by fire— I have no anger for their divergences; only let them know, let them love, let them remember.

Expressions of similarly deep religious piety may be found in the philosophical writings of the sophisticated Seneca, who can speak of God as a father and men as brothers. Cicero spoke of Jupiter as king of gods and men and all but identifies him with the stoic Logos. The philosopher Plutarch voices a view which was common to the philosophers as well as the mystery faiths when he says:

Not different gods among different peoples—gods of Barbarians, of Greeks, of the South, or of the North; but even as sun and moon, heaven and earth and sea are common to all, yet have different names along different peoples, so there is one Intelligence which rules in the world, one Providence which directs it; the same powers act everywhere. Honors, names, and symbols vary.

VII

How far the religious turn taken by philosophers of the early Roman Empire was due to the influence of a widely dispersed Judaism it is impossible to say. That it had some significance seems highly probable when one compares Epictetus and Seneca with early Christian teachers. But there were other forces which made thought more interested in the practical bearing of religion. It is usual for periods in which there are marked social expansion and rapid economic and political change to develop interest in ethics and religion. The new conditions tend to break down inherited inhibitions and sanctions, and the gods of the forefathers are no longer feared. It is natural for those who have found the changes to their advantage and who represent the privileged classes to look with concern on the threatened collapse of the social order on which they depend. They begin to worry about men's faith in God. Though they themselves may feel superior to such need, if their temper is critical and satirical they will insist upon the political necessity of popular religion, and like Pliny repair the local shrines. But in such days there appear men with something of the prophet's attitude who seek to turn men's attention to God and so stabilize their morals. This cycle of social change—the disintegration of morality, distrust of God, lamentation of the serious-minded, insistence upon new religious faith, reaffirmation of the religious basis for morals, attempted moral stabilization on the level of new social conditions—may be seen after every period where the mold of the past is broken. So it was in Europe after the Crusades, the rise of overseas commerce, and the discovery of America; so it was in France in the eighteenth century and in all the world in our day. Especially was it true in the case of

Rome, where the very greatness of the success of the Republic and the Empire brought about important social and economic readjustments.

There is no warrant for interpreting the pictures of the Roman Empire drawn by satirists as representing universal moral decadence. On the contrary, in the early Christian centuries the Empire was in the first stages of a development which was to continue until the fourth century at least. The transfer of vast quantities of booty from the East to Rome and the West, made possible the remarkable physical development in Italy and as in the course of time wealth moved backward to the East, built up the great cities on the frontier of the Empire in Syria. It was a period of widespread education, with universities and independent teachers. It is true that the morals among the wealthy classes had naturally suffered and those of the proletarian of the great cities were sensual. The development of moral ideals and a sense of the worth of the human personality were naturally checked by the presence of slavery and the exclusion of citizens from larger political affairs, but one has only to look at the inscriptions on the gravestones to realize that there was in the Empire of the first three Christian centuries a middle class of men and women leading self-respecting lives, and endeavoring to practice the virtues which society recognized. The spread of the mystery religions, the popularity of the teachers of morals, the increase in numbers of those who treated classical paganism as a convention and sought religious satisfactions in association with Judaism, all show that there was a quickening of the intellectual and moral life—a new turning to deity for aid in facing problems of life and thought arising from an increasingly complicated civilization. The Christian movement came into the Roman Empire not in a moment of despondency and degeneracy, but in one of social growth and intellectual expansion. The conception of God which this great period contributed to the new religion was born not of social decadence but of the needs of new social life.

Yet as the Olympian gods were seen to be incapable of ministering to this highly developed social order, there came upon the Roman Empire a sense of human need and weakness not far removed from pessimism. The folk religion became increasingly a means for avoiding ill-fortune, but the Olympians were incapable of removing from men a sense of ill-desert and of promising deliverance from death. Pictures of the underworld grew more distinct, but the hope of enjoying their imagined blessings grew faint. Intellectual men and women gained serenity from their philosophy, but even they, despite the exhortations of men like Epictetus, have left us few traces of religious joy. To the common people even such satisfactions were denied. They were face to face with an ineffective polytheism.

This sense of inefficiency was naturally deepened by the absence of political responsibility and the cultivation of an attitude of submission to the imperial rule. Without the stimulus of the opportunity for reform which modern life gives, it is not strange that great numbers of people looked to another type of religion which for centuries had been more or less present in Greek life, but which, with the absorption of the Near East into the Empire, spread with great rapidity. The new religions had savior gods. They promised the discouraged and disillusioned man participation in the experiences of the divinity itself. The mystery religions thus furnished the inspiration which a subject world demanded. The gods could do what man no longer felt capable of doing, that is, bring salvation.

There is no evidence that mystery religions, though similar, had any common ancestor. They all seem to have been regarded as satisfying the deeper questionings and sense of moral impotence to which the gods of mythology gave no response. They arose from observation of death and the procession of the seasons. These phenomena were beyond any human control. The germ in the mystery religions was the reappearance in spring of that life which apparently had ceased in winter. Such a deliverance suggested the passionate hope of overcoming death. The revivifying powers of nature were identified with some god or goddess who had been subject to death, but who had risen from the dead. Mythologies were dramatized into a religious technique by which the powers of nature became the powers for the transformation of the individual. Religious communities were formed of those who, by an elaborate ceremony of initiation, had come to share the revived life of the god. Mortality was thus succeeded by immortality. Since the initiations were secret our knowledge of their details is of course incomplete, but we know enough about some of their elements to enable us to see that they all served the same function: in some way the vivifying powers of the god were transferred to the initiate. Nor was this change merely superficial. As we know from the extraordinary ritual of *taurobolium* it was regarded as a rebirth. The symbolic acts of initiation had actual transforming significance. This transformation was to be followed by a better sort of life on the part of the initiate, and an entrance into a sacred fellowship. Morality was thus more or less connected with the new life given by union with a god. The initiation into a mystery religion was paganism's equivalent of a modern revival.

The gods of the classical religions made little or no moral appeal to the worshipers; the god of philosophy appealed to those choice spirits of mankind who searched for truth or self-control; the deified emperor was the God of an empire; the God of the prophets was the Father of a nation rather than the individual; but in the mystery religions the gods were the saviors of individuals, be they never so humble. One by one men and women through their initiation participated in the experience of a god who had died and been raised. They, too, as they believed, were delivered from the control of death. The mystery religions were something more than orgies or superstitions. They were the attempts to come into conscious help-gain relationship with the cosmic activities by a particular behavior. The attempt brought a new enthusiasm and exaltation. Whatever their excesses, the mystery religions were a dramatic expression of the belief that the individual had become identified with a god and so was regenerated and saved.

In an age that had outgrown its inherited gods and like all prosperous ages paradoxically felt the worthlessness of life, the inadequacy of philosophy, the inaccessibility of high ideals of the moralists, and the impotence of conventional religion to stir emotions, it was natural that these mystery religions, with their drama and assurance of immortality through union with the divine, should have spread widely and rapidly. Especially did the mysteries of Mithra appeal to soldiers, merchants, and travelers. But throughout the entire Empire there were groups who turned to the Great Mother Cybele, to Isis, to Dionysus, to Attis, as saviors from death and as the donors of a spiritual elevation hitherto claimed exclusively by the philosophers. Religious behavior is always easier than religious thought, and the mystery religion embodied the apparently indestructible belief that through some sacramental union with the divine men and women can gain divine qualities.

Furthermore, since these mystery religions had a common function, they came to be regarded as phases of the worship of a single God under different names. Thus they aided the trend toward religious unity which we have already seen was in the philosophy and the political religion of the Empire. Their followers felt that a common divine nature was manifested in all savior gods. Thus there appeared an unsystematized monotheism which expressed in the variety of cults the sense of cosmic unity which philosophy expressed. Theoretically, at least, any one of the gods of the mysteries might serve as the supreme God. Thus Apuleius represents the goddess Isis appearing to the hero of the *Metamorphoses* and saying:

To my divinity, one in itself, the entire world does reverence under many forms, with varied rites, and manifold names. Hence it is that the primal Phrygians call me at Pessinus the Mother of the Gods, hence the Athenians, who are sprung from the ground on which they dwell, name me Cecropian Minerva, the wave-beat Cyprians Paphian Venus, the archer Cretans Dictynnan Diana, the Sicilians with their triple speech Stygian Proserpina, the people of Eleusis ancient Ceres, others Juno, others Bellona, some Hecate, again Rhamnusia; but the Æthiopians on whom shine the rays of the sun at his birth, the Arians, and the Egyptians, mighty in their ancient learning, worship me with the proper rites and call me by my true name Queen Isis.

VIII

Thus the historical process which had given rise to a social unity typified by the worship of the Emperor was paralleled by a tendency toward religious unity represented by the attempted universalizing of a single Olympian or mystery god and by the discovery of a metaphysical unity lying behind all natural processes. Monotheism of a genuine sort was thus foreshadowed, but it would have been impossible, so long as there was no social group capable of synthesizing the elements diversely expressed by the different trends within the Roman Empire. Belief in a single God so essential to tribal unity in primitive religion, but obscured in the eclectic appropriations of polytheism, was to express itself more intelligently in Western civilization. For within the expanding group of Christians, depressed as proletarian, prosecuted as revolutionists and atheists, and contemned as ignorant and unphilosophical, there was to evolve a unified conception of God. Attempts to maintain the integrity of the group and an identity of attitude among its members were to lead to a expanded idea of God in which all the monotheistic currents of the West and of Judaism were united.

CHAPTER V

THE RISE OF CHRISTIAN MONOTHEISM

THUS there developed in the midst of the polytheism in what we provincially call the ancient world two chief monotheisms, one religious and the other metaphysical. Each was calculated to supplement the other. If the Hebrew monotheism lacked a philosophy, the monotheism of Greek philosophers lacked the religious appeal. Each was the outcome of centuries of human effort, but neither was capable of furnishing a religious motive for others than its authors. The monotheism of the Jew was religious, and was limited to a cult and a race. The monotheism of the Greek was the product of the philosophically minded citizens of an empire. Under the influence of the mystery religions the two fused in Christianity.

I

This union was not planned; indeed, one might almost say it was unexpected, due to the change in personnel of the Christian community. The original Christian group was composed of Jews who attached a Jewish interpretation to their leader Jesus, justified their loyalty to him as a Jewish Christ by appealing to the Jewish Scripture, never detached themselves from the Jewish religion, and looked forward to a divinely established Jewish empire. When those who were not Jews joined the group, tension arose between the two parties. All had a similar loyalty to

Jesus as the Christ; all had had the same religious experience; all had been baptized. But the original Jewish body demanded conformity in cult. The gentile Christian must become a Jew. Thanks to the influence of Paul, the Gentiles were freed from the observance of the law. Even without Paul any other outcome would have been improbable. New converts from the Hellenistic world were not joining Judaism but a new movement in which they could enjoy a salvation wrought by God and as vividly experienced as in the mystery religions. A Jewish-Gentile union was, however impracticable. If Christians so nearly identical as some of our modern denominations find it impossible to meet at the Lord's table, how much more difficult it must have been for Jewish and non-Jewish Christians to maintain any sort of unity. The Jew disappeared from the new movement, but he left in it his Bible, his messiah, and his God. Christians became a Hellenistic religious group under the control of Jewish monotheism. Or, to put the matter in another way, within the Christian community there was brought about the fusion of the two racial monotheisms. The God of the Bible became the God of philosophy, and the God of philosophy became the God of the Bible.

II

The process of the combination of the Hebrew and Aryan streams of monotheism into a single concept was due to the interaction of groups of individuals through the lines of commerce and trades. A picture of the Roman Empire of the early Christian centuries would show a remarkable interpenetration of peoples. The breakdown of national exclusiveness had removed checks from travel and great cities like Alexandria, Ephesus, and especially

Rome, were filled with men and women from all quarters of the Empire. In fact, in some cases they were so numerous as to form considerable sections of a city. The migration seems to have been then, as now, from the East to the West. There was to come a time when the Northern tribes were to move south across the northern frontier of the Empire, but that was after the economic forces of the Empire had broken down. From the days of Augustus to those of Constantine, at least, migrations were of individuals or small groups who carried with them elements of their own cultures and religions. So it came to pass that the Empire became a battleground of new rival religions, all of them derived from the East and all of them being to a greater or less degree institutionalized in some group of believers.

Probably the most significant of these groups was that of the Jews who swarmed throughout the cities of the Empire, engaged in various trades and business undertakings. By the first Christian century Palestine had ceased to be either the exclusive home of the Jews or exclusively populated by Jews. The little land, filled though it was with towns and cities, was quite incapable of caring for the increasing number of the total Jewish population. There grew up a dispersion of the Jews from Palestine just as there later grew up a migration of the Irish from Ireland, and for much the same reasons. The Jews enjoyed favors given them by Cæsar for the aid given him by Herod, and Judaism was a licensed religion, although the Roman gentry had difficulty in understanding the peculiarities of the Jewish communities, especially their observations of the sabbath and their refusal to eat pork.

The Jews differed from other religious groups in a variety of ways, but perhaps in none more markedly than

in the fact that in the place of temples they built synagogues wherein the roll of the Law was the center of
honor and there was no sacrifice or statue of a god. The
Jews had no mysteries. Their feasts were open to observation, and in the case of proselytes there was no initiatory
drama with its symbols. Indeed, in the cases of some of
these proselytes circumcision was not required. Judaism's
holy scriptures were revered as divinely inspired. Unlike
other religious groups, too, the Jews had not only a
single god to whom they were fanatically loyal, but also
communications from that god which they attempted to
embody in their conduct and hope. The fact that they
were not only a religious but an ethnic group, to which
entrance usually could be gained only by a painful ceremony, doubtless prevented Judaism from becoming a missionary or a universal religion. It is, however, clear that
its monotheism, whose evolution we have traced, was a
distinct contribution to the development of the idea of
God among non-Jews. Thanks to the inscriptions we can
now see how influential the Jewish communities became
among the non-Jewish peoples. Their monotheism and the
observation of the sabbath appealed to many persons, and
there grew up a sort of penumbral religious group known
as the "pious ones," who did not take over the entire cult
of Judaism but did take over its belief in one god. They
also seem to have shared to some extent in the Jewish
hope for the new age. How deeply this hope had pene-
trated Roman thought can be seen in the recasting of the
Jewish Sibylline Oracles in the *Fourth Eclogue* of Virgil.

These informal associations in which Jews associated
on more or less equality with those who were not Jews
furnished social contacts by which the monotheism of the
Jew and the philosophical interest of the Gentiles became,

as it were, mutually contagious. Thus the synthesis of the two monotheisms was begun. No new religious group or movement resulted, but Gentiles were gradually drawn into the Jewish communities. The historical significance of these monotheists lay chiefly in that they prepared a group of Gentiles to organize Christian Judaism into an independent religion with its own conceptions of God and salvation.

III

Within Judaism there was one group that believed that the Messiah, that is to say, the one in whom was embodied the saving spirit of God, had appeared in the person of Jesus of Nazareth. From this faith there was to evolve a unique idea of God. The first step was to regard Jesus as the possessor of divinity.

Incarnation was foreign to the Hebrew thought, but power through spiritual unction was its non-biological equivalent. The followers of Jesus listened to his teaching, but their primary interest was in his death and resurrection, as an example and revelation of the divine salvation. The proportion of material in the gospel narratives indicates this central concern. The gospel which Paul told the Corinthians he had received had to do with the death and resurrection of the Christ. He almost never refers to a teaching of the Master, but he does recall the Supper which was developing into a Christian rite. The accounts of the deeds and teaching of Jesus were illustrations of the manner in which the divine power which could triumph over death expressed itself in human relations. That divine power had also been present in his brief public career. By the finger of God he had cast out demons and so vanquished the kingdom of evil, and by

God's spirit had taught with authority beyond that of the ordinary teacher.

Any fair reading of the New Testament will show that the Christian community almost, if not quite, from its very start looked upon Jesus as possessed of superhuman —one might indeed say supernatural powers. The Christian movement took form and grew around this conception. Men did not accept him merely as a teacher but as a Messiah who had expressed his messianic power in teaching. What was more, he had given his followers the same spirit of power which he possessed. He had risen from the community of the dead in Sheol and had ascended to heaven, from which any day he might be expected to return. Pending that return, he had sent the spirit of God to the community he had left. That the early disciples respected the teaching of Jesus is evident in the existence of the gospels themselves, but their community was not that of a school of thought or of social reform, but that of a religion which added to the practices and beliefs of Judaism this new faith as to Jesus. Our synoptic gospels in their present form are the outcome of this interpretation.

The early stages of the Christian community cannot be understood by desupernaturalizing this conception of Jesus first expressed in the messianic pattern. If the Jews had been polytheists it is easy to imagine that a being possessed of the Spirit of God might have been erected into a God. But Hebrew monotheism made that impossible. Yet the new experiences, the ecstasies, the glossolalia, the power to work cures, which followed their acceptance of Jesus as Christ were attributed by Christians immediately to the working of the Spirit which he had sent them from his place of authority in heaven. It was impossible for him to remain on the level of the prophet or the teacher. So long as the community was composed of Jews, the messianic definition was enough, but when it was composed of those who were not Jews, messiahship had to be explained and revalued for the benefit of the new members of the church. The stages of this process can be seen in the letters of Paul. To him Jesus had been set forth by the Spirit of God as the Christ by being raised from the dead. But the divine power of the messianic office grew increasingly prominent. With his belief in preëxistence, Paul thought of Jesus as "The man from heaven." He had no theory as to how the Christ became flesh unless it be in his exhortation to the Christians at Philippi to emulate Jesus' humility in "emptying" himself. He who had been in the form of God, instead of seeking full equality with God, had humbled himself and become a man, and even submitted to the death on the cross. Because of his humbleness God had highly exalted him and given him a supreme place in all creation.

Nor did Pauline thought stop there. The apostle had both his formal and his experiential conception of Christianity. On the one side Jesus was to be the Messiah by whom the kingdom of God was to be established. When men had accepted him as the Christ who had been raised from the dead, they came into the favored position of children of God. They might therefore look forward with confidence to acquittal at the coming Judgment Day when Jesus himself was to be the judge. He could not be expected to condemn his brethren. This aspect of his gospel was purely formal, the utilization of the Jewish pattern, and was outside the area of experience. The real center of the Pauline thought was his belief that those who had this loyalty to the Messiah received his spirit and became new creatures in Christ. They possessed moral motives which were the gift of the spirit. It was this newness of life that argued the prospective acquittal. And Paul attributed it both directly and indirectly to Jesus the Christ.

It was natural that Paul should have appropriated something from the mystery religions. Doubtless many of the new converts to his gospel of salvation had known or joined some mystery cult. To call Jesus Lord was to use the designation of the mystery cults for a Savior-God. The Lord was the Spirit who wrought the new creation in men's lives. Paul unhesitatingly speaks of being baptized into Christ, of putting Christ on, of being crucified with Christ, of being raised with Christ, and living the risen life of Christ. In these expressions the historical Jesus became a divine being. Because of his non-philosophical turn of mind Paul does not seem to have been conscious of the metaphysical difficulties which this view involved. He clung steadily to his Hebrew monotheism and believed that ultimately, after the Christ had conquered all the enemies of God including death, he would deliver authority to God who would then be all in all.

Such teachings would of necessity among Greek minds demand some sort of philosophical explication and adjustment to monotheism, but against this Paul protested vehemently. He insisted that love, not knowledge, was the center of the new life. For it expressed in human relations the love of God which had already streamed into the hearts of the reborn Christians. He told the Corinthians, who seem to have been truly Greek in their curiosity to draw conclusions from the premises of the new religion, that knowledge puffed up; that it was love that built up. He did not undertake to disillusion the Christians of Asia Minor, who were inclined to those theosophies and mystery religions which were later to give rise to the Gnostic movement. He simply told them that God had "chaptered up" all things in Christ, including the miscellaney of supernatural powers and beings they were tempted to worship. Christ was not an afterthought of God but his work was planned before creation and through him God had created the world.

A further stage in this religious elevation of Christ to a more than human station appears in the Fourth Gospel. There his capacity to function as a representative of God was explained as due to the fact that he was the incarnate Logos. This was carrying the Lord of Paul into the very heart of the Greek speculative thought. While, it is true, the Logos conception is formally expressed only in its opening phrases, the entire Fourth Gospel is an exposition of Jesus as the Son of God, the giver of eternal life. An attitude toward him was an attitude toward God. He was the way to the Father. Nay, he who had seen him had seen the Father. One after another of the messianic expectations of the primitive church were spiritualized without being abandoned until at last the second coming of the Christ itself is said to be the spiritual reception of the Father and the Son by those who follow the teachings of Jesus. It was this conception of the Fourth Gospel that naturally appealed to the Greek thought, for it was the reëxpression of the messianic significance of Jesus in Greek terms, far more philosophical than the unsystematized, exuberant appreciation of Paul. And it was the Christ of the Fourth Gospel that after the first century led to the organization of the theology of the church, composed exclusively of Hellenists and Romans.

It would be incorrect to regard Jesus as thus reinterpreted as a substitute for the God of Hebraism. That conception of God was never abandoned. A more accurate statement would be that the group of monotheists constituting the early Christian church had found Jesus so central in their Christian life as unconsciously to respond to the polytheistic mind-set which characterized the world of which they were a part. They would not be polytheists, but neither did they shrink from attributing to Jesus the function of God in the creation of the world, and the giving of divine life to men. The Logos, the Son of God, had become flesh and in so doing had, to use the expression of Irenæus, theized humanity. By the incarnation the Logos had become what men were in order that he might make them what he had been, that is, possessed of complete immortality. Such religious conceptions were to become the breeding place of metaphysical problems.

Another influence of the Greek thought in elevating Jesus to divine eminence is to be seen in the belief that he had been miraculously born of a virgin. The Jewish Christian could speak of Jesus as the Son of God because the term simply connoted messianic dignity and power. But to the church, when once it had become composed of adult Gentiles accustomed to the idea of the descendants of gods and human beings, the term early came to mean the absence of an earthly father. The earliest type of accepted tradition attributed the power of Jesus to the coming of the divine Spirit upon him at his baptism. By the end of the first century these two conceptions of messianic sonship and the transforming presence of the Spirit had been united, and Jesus as the Son of God was said to have been conceived by the Holy Spirit. Such a view has from that day been regarded as essential by Christian orthodoxy. It is difficult, if not impossible, to combine it logically with later trinitarianism. If the Son of Mary had been said to have been conceived by God, the Father, the difficulty would not arise. But the incarnate Son of God had two fathers. The Eternal Son had God the Father and the human Jesus had the Holy Spirit. Augustine suggested but evaded this conclusion. Intellectual confusion always arises from an attempt to treat a pattern as a scientific fact.

<h2 style="text-align:center">IV</h2>

The fact is that, as McGiffert in his *God of the Early Christians* has shown, there was developing in the Christian movement a new divinity. At the same time the movement was perpetuating a synthetic monotheism. So long as there was no general organization of Christians or any authoritatively accepted formula of that for which it stood, the struggle between these two tendencies would be inevitable. It was a situation that nobody could have anticipated, due, as it was, to the development of a new religion centering around the acceptance of Jesus as a divine savior by converts accustomed to polytheism. Within the community of Christians intense loyalty and faith in their new Lord led many to treat him as a God. Indeed, the term itself is applied to him. By the beginning of the second century Ignatius on his way to martyrdom longs "to attain unto Jesus Christ," and to be "an imitator of the passion of my God." Pliny in his famous letter to Trajan said the Christian offered prayer to Christ as to a divinity. Justin Martyr could call the incarnate Logos "another God" and the apocryphal writings of the time, like the Acts of Thomas, spoke of him as a new God. It would be easy to multiply passages illustrating the fact that in gentile communities there was a readiness to accept Jesus as a new mystery god. Indeed, this likeness is used by some of the apologists as a sort of *ad hominem* argument against their critics. Such an apotheosis was of course natural when one recalls that great numbers of Christians could have had no intelligent knowledge of the Bible and even less of current philosophy. Accustomed as they were to take over new gods, they had no difficulty in accepting Jesus in place of the gods of their multitudinous polytheism.

But such ascription of divinity to Jesus was by no means universal. The Christian movement as a whole was rooted in something more than the mystery faith. It had the divine oracles which set forth the Hebrew God, and it had the philosophy of the schools which could think of the incarnation of Divine Reason. Clear thinkers like Clement of Alexandria never erected Jesus into a God. To them he was the incarnation of the Logos who revealed the absolute God in human experience. The Christian had more than faith, he had a new knowledge.

Clement's exposition of the significance of the Logos to human morals and good manners must have been too recondite for the popular mind. But his philosophy and the Hebrew Scriptures saved him from genuine polytheism, and he worshiped not a human character but a God who was being revealed in that character. Origen, the successor of Clement in the school at Alexandria, in representing the belief of the Christian community as a whole, denied the charge Celsus had made long before, that Jesus was a God. According to Origen the Christians did not pray to Jesus but to God in the name of Jesus. His acute mind, dominated as it was by a philosophical as well as a biblical monotheism, could not endure the popular christological polytheism of the Christian sects.

By the second century, therefore, the Christian community was called upon to choose between a monotheism whose God had revealed himself in Jesus and a polytheism which did not hesitate to ascribe to Jesus actual divinity. Obviously such a contrast was more than academic. The real character of the new religion was at stake. There was difficulty whichever horn of the dilemma was chosen. If the biblical and philosophical monotheism were to triumph, there was danger lest Jesus, as with some of the Ebionites, should become an ordinary historical character without any of the qualities of the Savior Christians had discovered. If, on the other hand, Jesus were to be the sole Savior-God of the Christians, the Christian movement would have little to distinguish it from other mystery religions of the time. The teachers of the church became conscious of this antithesis and endeavored in some way to resolve it. The solution of the difficulty, however, did not come from philosophy but by the social development of a formula and mode of thought to which the Christian community became accustomed and accepted as a test of membership within itself. In the process of such development of orthodoxy, the practices of the church which really constituted much of the religion of its members served to conserve the divine quality given Jesus.

The struggle with the Gnostics sharpened the biblical theism the movement conserved. The location of the divine Jesus Christ in a philosophical world-view was one of the earliest attempts of the Christian movement. Some settled the matter offhand by saying that his humanity was only a phantasm from which the divine Christ separated himself on the cross. For God, they held, could not suffer. But good sense and the gospels prevailed and the Docetic was regarded as a heretic untrue to the revelation of inspired Scriptures. But speculation in a Hellenistic world could not be checked. The new religion needed a cosmology. The Christian community was not a body of technical philosophers, but had within it a large proportion of men who attempted some sort of philosophizing. In this it resembled the church of our modern world. The plain Christian has always been more responsive to the picturesque vagaries of amateur thinking than to the severely logical discussion of his own terms. The Gnostic movement embodied something more than a vagary. Composed as it was, of various groups with their different teachers and systems, it had a common basis. In so far as its followers became Christians, it was a prescientific attempt to subsume the Christian religion in a cosmological worldview. The Hellenistic world, continually raising the question as to the origin of the universe and the relation of spirit and matter, lacked the data supplied by modern physical and biological sciences. It turned to a crude forecast of evolution and saw the cosmos as ruled by emanation and generation. The ultimate was not defined, but was Depth or Abyss. From it emanated a variety of more or less personified abstractions like Truth and Mind. From these couples there were all sorts of descendants which finally included a demiurge and Jesus.

We know the Gnostic movement by its literary remains, but more completely in the elaborate criticism of Irenæus. Its systems seem to the modern mind incoherent and fantastic, but when one really examines the purpose of this Gnosis, it is evident that it is one of those ever recurring attempts of men to discover a unifying world-view in which religion shall be one element. It was inevitable that this ambitious effort should distinguish sharply between the beneficent Father of Jesus and the Hebrew God who had created what seemed a heartless universe. This

God with all other Hebrew beliefs Gnostics rejected. It was the same sort of antithesis that appears in Zoroastrianism, Christian Science, theosophy, and that modern philosophy of religion which completely separates the sphere of science from the sphere of religion.

In the light of the history of human thought there is no denying the attractiveness of this dualism. The really serious question which every religion has been forced to face is whether any adjustment of nature and God is possible. The Hindu and the Buddhist frankly say there is not so long as human life is in the causal sequence of Karma. For them the only salvation is Nirvana in which individuality is lost in cosmic happiness. The Christian church, however, could make no such answer and survive. It carried forward the teachings of prophet and philosopher. But Gnosticism was to leave its influence upon the beliefs of the growing Church. A divine triad of Father, Mother, Son, emanating from the Ultimate, the dualism of spirit and matter, identified with good and evil, the cosmological significance of the Christ, the mystery of sacraments, all aided the reshaping of the rising Christian theology.

But even more important was the challenge Gnosticism gave the as yet unsystematized theism. Could the Savior-God and the Father-God of Christians be identified with the Creator-God? A negative answer would have meant the end of the developing monotheism. The various Gnostic schools might ultimately have yielded to ridicule and fallen of the weight of their own analogies, but if they had succeeded in subsuming Christian thought in their world-view, the Christian religion would have shared the fate of Gnosticism itself. What really saved Christianity as an independent religion was the triumph of the enlarged biblical conception of God. Back of the Christian formulas lay the authority, not of a world-view, but of Scripture setting forth a God who was not only the creator and immanent reason of the universe but a loving Father. That was the historic faith of the entire Christian movement. In the light of the long struggle between a pseudo-science and a religious movement with an inspired literature, a creator, a divine Founder-Savior, a revealed God, and a developing organization, the first sentence of the ancient symbols and their descendant creeds was glorious audacity. For it declared that Christians believed in God the Father, maker of heaven and earth. The God of love revealed by Jesus was the God of nature set forth by philosophers. The transforming Spirit of Paul was the regenerating God of the mysteries. Again the idea of God had expanded as men with new needs and new patterns faced problems set by nature as well as human weakness.

V

Yet this recognition of love and creative power in God left the divine Jesus still a problem. Should he like other gods in the Empire, be worshiped without being regarded as a supreme god? The Christian community had in some way to adjust him to the God who had made heaven and earth and who was to be found by philosophy rather than by history. He was subordinate to the Father, said Origen and his followers. But in what sense subordinate? In office, said some; in substance, said others. On the one side was the monotheism of the Bible and of the Greco-Roman world; on the other side was the conviction that salvation from death had come through an incarnate Logos who had been raised from the dead and through his incarnation had brought the divine and human natures into contact. This contact was more than theoretical. By it human nature, not merely an individual, had been raised from the dead. A conviction of full personal immortality was the dominant need of Hellenist Christians. They had long practiced baptism in the name of the Father, Son, and Spirit, and their baptismal font was known as the "laver of immortality." But God alone was the source of immortality. If real God had not affected real human nature, the religious practices and beliefs of the Christian were mistaken and futile. Their souls might be immortal but their personality after death would be incomplete. They would have no bodies. But if real divine nature had been incarnate in real human nature then the flesh as well as the spirit had been given immortality.

The issue, therefore, sprang from a religious tension. It could not be avoided. If the Logos Son, was a creature, real God had not touched human nature. If he were in any other way different in substance from the Father the entire Christian scheme of salvation was demolished and the new religion had become a polytheism.

There was another problem in the terminology of the Hebrew scriptures, the divine oracles. They spoke of one God but they also spoke of the Father, the Son, and the Holy Spirit. How such a terminology was consistent with monotheism seems never to have troubled the Hebrew. His interest in Jahweh had never been metaphysical. But to the church of the third century the issue was real. How could there be one God at the same time a Father, a Son, and a Spirit? How could an individual be treated as a God and yet there be a God-substance that was universal and a divine reason that was in all natural processes?

And how could divine substance have a spirit? Were there three gods? Were there four gods? Did the Father suffer? Did the Son have a beginning?

Such questions as these are far enough from the practical interests of later days, but they were vastly significant to the men of the fourth century. Little opportunity was given for anything except private interests in the Roman Empire. Any organization attempting to forward social, much less political reform, would have been immediately subject, as were the Christians, to persecution. Trajan would not even permit a fire company to be organized in Nicomedia. Yet the Greco-Roman world was intellectually alert. The rise of the Christian church gave it issues which, until the time of Constantine, were quite independent of politics or social problems. Metaphysical discussion was by no means limited to the theologian. At first, it is true, the more simple-minded Christians looked with some anxiety at the attempt of such men as Clement of Alexandria to introduce philosophy into the exposition of the gospel. Tertullian was especially outspoken in his belief that the heretics, so to speak, had no standing in court because they did not accept the gospel as final, but wished to get new truth through philosophy. "But what fellowship," he cried, "have Athens and Jerusalem? What likeness is there between a philosopher and a Christian; between a disciple of Greece and a disciple of heaven?" As time passed these questions of interpretation and philosophical explanations of Christian formulas led to the formation of parties and party cries. Discussion of the most elusive matters was replaced by the slogans of partisanship. The very cobblers of Constantinople were discussing the generation of the Son, and the stevedores of Egypt were singing the hymns of Arius. Only as we remember that the issues raised by Christian thought were within the limits of permissible discussion and that the developing Christian movement offered opportunity for the organization of parties and sects on the basis of theological interests, can we understand how the excitement which in modern times centers around political issues and political parties could have been centered upon the metaphysical discussions as to the nature of the Godhead before the universe was created.

As it was, the first attempt at theoretically unifying the various elements of the Christian belief about God was the use of an analogy which by virtue of general use became a pattern. This analogy, though perhaps not original with him, was not furnished by a philosopher but by Tertullian, a lawyer, to whom we owe not a few of the important legal words in an orthodox theological vocabulary. Roman law had taken over a term which originally belonged to the drama. The actor had been accustomed to wear a mask to play his different characters, and one actor might therefore appear in several disguises or *personæ*. The use of this latter term in law meant the capacity in which a man appeared in the court. The same man might in one court be a creditor, in another a debtor, in another a criminal. As an individual he was the same, but in his relations and activities he had various *personæ*. Tertullian used this figure in reference to God. The Father, the Son, and the Spirit, he said, were the three *personæ* of the God-substance. He did not discuss the matter in ways that would have been altogether satisfactory in the fourth century, for he came near the heretical thought of Sabellius that God had modes of revelation, but he gave the church a terminology which was to continue. There was one God-substance existing in three *personæ*.

This was to be the center of new discussion because the Latin and Greek terms used were not exactly identical. The Latin word *substantia* was employed for one of the meanings of the Greek word *essence* (*ousia*), and the Latin word *personæ* for the Greek word *hypostasis*, which etymologically was identical with *substance*. But this confusion of terms was after all only incidental to the attempt on the part of speculative minds of the Hellenistic world to discover the exact relationship of those *personæ* to each other and to the God-substance itself. The inhibition against discussions of more practical matters served to make such discussion the basis for group rivalries which in the beginning of the fourth century in the mind of Constantine threatened the peace of the Empire itself. The final formula of the orthodox view of God was born of this party struggle far more than of the triumph of theological logic or of the arguments of theological disputants. In vocabulary and in authority the trinitarian doctrine was a striking illustration of the way in which an analogy by virtue of widespread social usage becomes a pattern of thought. What is regarded as the most, if not the only, genuinely metaphysical dogma of the Christian religion is thus in fact a development of a social practice given metaphysical standing by political as well as by church authority. It is a formula of group attitude.

But the real heart of the doctrine of the Trinity was not in its metaphysics, but in another pattern in good standing among Christians of all parties. That was the pattern of paternity. When first the Christian movement was given cultural expression by the great teachers of

Alexandria, it promised to be a development of the Stoic-Platonic doctrine of the Logos so popular in the city of Philo. The reader of the works of Clement of Alexandria can never avoid speculation as to what might have been the course of Christian thought if this term had remained central in christological discussion. But it was too abstract for the popular mind, and by the third century it had been pretty generally replaced by the term "Son of God" who had been begotten by the Father. Such a pattern was not only scriptural but, until seriously discussed, easily grasped.

Philosophy was abandoned and the metaphysical problem of the position of the divine Christ in the Godhead was assuaged—one can hardly say answered—by the new use of an old pattern, generation. As the son is in origin of the same material as the father, so Christ as the Son of God could be said to have been begotten. The logical difficulty with such an answer to a philosophical question was precisely what Arius pointed out; however much a son might be said to be of the same substance as the father, the mere fact that he was begotten argued that there was a time when he was not begotten. This simple fact made the Son, however like the Father, and however he might be worshiped as Creator and Lord, of a different substance from the Father, a creature. The Father was timeless, the Son was in time. Origen, long before the discussion had become a threat to the unity of the Empire, had met this argument by the assertion that the divine Son was not in time. To use his term, the generation was eternal. Obviously what he meant to say was that the pattern could not be taken as more than an analogy of that which it actually expressed. But the literal use of a pattern brought new difficulties. Who was the eternal Son's mother? Heretics said the Holy Ghost. The church never took the matter seriously, although apologists for trinitarianism have argued that if God is to be love, *personæ* are necessary just as complete family love argues two parents and a child. The pattern of generation, however, was capable of expressing one aspect of the Father-Son relation found in the vocabulary of Hebrews who never dreamed of a metaphysical trinity, namely, the Son and Father must be of the same substance, not merely of like substance.

The real problem set the Council of Nicea was that of finding how three could be treated as one rather than how one could be treated as three. So long as the discussion was on the level of biblical language the question was really not metaphysical but literary. But despite all the praise which has been given the Greeks because of their devotion to art, when it came to religious thought they were not content to deal with images. Analogies of philosophical truths were substituted for the statues of the Olympian gods. The Son was begotten, not made—a formula to which the Arians would assent—but of the same substance—a term that the Arians would not use.

But discussion did not cease. A pattern could put three into one, but the Greek theologians were not satisfied to let it remain even in the tautological formulas of the original Nicene creed. They wanted metaphysics, not patterns. At once they began to discuss what was really meant by identity of substance between the Father and the Son. Not even the state could stop the argument. The outcome of the discussion would probably have shocked Athanasius. On the one hand were the university-bred thinkers of Cappadocia—Basil, Gregory of Nyssa, and Gregory Nazianzen—who saw tritheism threatening in the new orthodoxy. To them the Son could be said to be of the same substance as the Father because he had qualities similar to those of the Father. Such a sensible formula was not vivid enough for the Christian masses. They could understand generation, but a Son whose identity of substance with the Father was the possession of qualities like the Father's was too refined a conception. They would rather have the doctrine of the Trinity a mystery than described in words which were neither Athanasian nor Arian. And so it has remained—an object of faith beyond the reach of wisdom, to be accepted on the basis of authority and defended by the use of analogies and anathemas. The orthodox mind has always wanted to eliminate a defined wrong in order to believe an undefined opposite that was correct. It is no mere accident that the Council of Nicea in its endeavor to exclude the Arians from the church by a term they would not use, made that term a test of orthodoxy, and attached anathemas to those who believed its contrary. Then, as always, it was easier to condemn than to convert.

The other outcome of the effort to treat metaphysically a pattern which had become a party slogan is seen in Augustine. He was too keen a thinker not to see the difficulty in the trinitarian formula, but as orthodox was bound to defend trinitarianism. The problem he faced, however, was the opposite of that faced by Athanasius. Three *personæ* had been given unity in a God-substance by orthodoxy. Augustine endeavored to see how one substance could exist in three *personæ*. In his effort to avoid the modal trinitarianism of the Sabellian heresy he really reduced trinitarianism to the God concept itself. He argued that since the *personæ* were of the substance and the substance could not be divided, it must act in its entirety whenever any *persona* acted. When the Father acted, the Son and the Spirit also acted. He thus concentrated attention upon God rather than upon trinitarian formula, for the only difference that Augustine apparently could discover between the *personæ* was that the Father was unbegotten, the Son was begotten, and the Holy Ghost proceeded.

It is no wonder that when Augustine wrote as a deeply religious soul rather than as an expounder of an orthodox doctrine that lay beyond reason, he spoke simply of God. "Two things," he said, "interest me, God and the soul." From his day to this the Trinity has been less the object of trust and aspiration than the God of Hebrew anthropomorphism enriched with the cosmic Being of philosophy.

The God of the Christian, however, has been more than a metaphysical problem or an abstraction. He has been personal. To this conception the trinitarian formula has contributed. For it served a profoundly religious need. It is quite unjust to say with Carlyle that men for centuries debated over a diphthong, that is to say, over the difference between the word *homousios,* of identical substance, and *homoiousios,* of a similar substance, as applied to the preexistent Son of God. There was a much more significant issue involved, namely, whether Christianity should succumb to the disintegrating forces of polytheism or in some way express the new sense of imperial unity and be correlated with Hebrew and Greek monotheism. Arianism was an unconscious reaction to polytheism. As a matter of fact, the question never was settled philosophically. What really took place was the authoritative adoption of a pattern which gave a new content to monotheism. The God-substance, existing in three *personæ,* or three personal relationships to nature, salvation, and human experience, finally became much more than the test of theological regularity. Trinitarianism was not speculative, but practical and religious. The one important thing which it gave the Greco-Roman mind was assurance that the Christian salvation was actually due to the transforming personal relationship of God and man. This, it is to be remembered, is the heart of religion as distinct from ethics, for every religion has attempted to express the possibility of gaining some assistance from personal relations with whatever a social group regards as divine. The Hebrew religion, the Christian worship of Jesus, the salvation dramatized in the mystery religion, the metaphysical conception of the Absolute of Plato and the Dynamic Reason of the Stoic were fused by the church into a new and unique conception of God.

The Trinity when seen historically is a functional concept, a pattern born of law and drama. Its value is vastly more than an authoritative answer to the metaphysical problems set by an outgrown philosophy. It not only enabled the Christian to avoid the high polytheism of divine triads found in other religions, but helped Greek minds under the authority of a Semitic theism to transform the metaphysical Absolute into a God who, when met in nature, or the experience of Jesus, or the experience of others, is as personal as Jahweh. Despite all efforts to reduce the divine to a process or a principle, the Christian movement centered around a God personally revealed and personally approached. The very intensity of the discussion as to natures led to new religious behavior. Men faced a mystery, but a mystery that was personal, not abstract or mechanistic. And therefore they worshiped and prayed to any one of the divine *personæ* that seemed most approachable.

But here a word of caution is needed. From the trinitarian point of view Jesus could be treated as God not because he was a man but because in his experience and person there was to be seen the presence of a God who in nature could be seen as a Father. Theological orthodoxy from the days of Tertullian has never undertaken to treat the humanity of Jesus as divine. That would be a denial of the metaphysical conception of unchangeable essences or substances or natures. But equally has it been affirmed that in his genuinely human nature there was working the same God that is to be seen in nature and in all religious experience. It would therefore be a distortion of the doctrine of the Trinity to say that it made a God out of a human being or a God into a human being. Popular theology has unfortunately neglected the religious element of the doctrine of the Trinity, for throughout the history of the Christian movement Jesus has functioned as a deity without any very careful distinction between the elements in his person which an orthodox creed like that of Chalcedon endeavored to protect. And it is probable that there has been altogether too much presentation of the doctrine of the Trinity as if it were a tritheism. But even the most unintelligent of orthodox expositors would deny that there were three gods. It is impossible to think scientifically about terms which are symbolical rather than defined. That the use of undefinable terms met the intellectual tension of an increasingly organized group was due less to philosophical argument than to religious usages and the authority of church and state. The Trinity became a pattern in a religion that in the experience and social behavior of its followers combined the monotheistic convictions of two racial histories.

CHAPTER VI

THE GOD OF CHRISTIAN THEOLOGY

THE evolution of the conception of God as a trinity of *personæ* was the work of an authoritative community of Christians. A social order dominated by imperialism could not have developed a democratic religious group. True, the early Christian communities are sometimes described as democracies, but such a description requires a new definition of democracy. The early Christian communities regarded themselves as supernaturally guided. They did not elect their first officials, but accepted them as divinely appointed. God had established a division of labor in the church by the gift of his Spirit, and apostles, prophets, teachers, evangelists, miracle-workers were selected by lot and as the choice of the Holy Spirit. As the communities multiplied and grew in power, the tendency toward authoritative organization became more marked. Doctrines became authoritative by the act of synods and councils. These bodies were at first local, but their decisions directly as well as indirectly affected the whole Christian movement. The decision of one council might be opposed by another, but each claimed to represent the mind of God and to set forth truth, which every Christian community should accept. Heresy was not only a divergence of religious belief, but also a group antagonism.

In an empire there could be only one way of dealing with such a situation. Unity had to be established. When once Constantine had come to believe that the supernatural powers represented by the Christian church were greater than those represented by heathen religions, he aligned himself with the church and counted upon the support of its Christ in battle and in administration. But he soon found that the Christian community had different conceptions of the Christ in whose sign he had conquered. The Empire was threatened with division which had its root in a difference of opinion as to the very supernatural power upon which he relied. His effort to get unity in belief led to the calling of the first ecumenical council of the church. There was then established a precedent which was to have a profound effect upon the development not only of the Christian community but on the Christian conception of God.

As might have been expected, the pattern of political unity was most developed in the western part of the Empire where imperialism had been creative rather than administrative as in the East. The development of the idea of God was thus conditioned by the political behavior of the two halves of the Empire. In the East there never appeared any imperial unity in the church, but a number of patriarchates differing little in authority, although naturally Constantinople was granted a certain amount of prestige. In the West, however, there was only one great city, and that was Rome.

I

The Eastern Empire had no social development which compelled the development of the idea of God beyond the point reached in the period when it had been intellectually alert and metaphysically interested. In Western Europe, however, the situation was radically different. If one were to chart the area within which Western civilization was developed, it would be found to be almost identical with that within which Latin Christianity developed. It is impossible, indeed, to understand the history of Western Christianity without reference to those centuries of economic and social debacle and reconstruction. The needs of Western Europe were not those of the philosopher but of the statesman and warrior. The religion which there developed was a religion of strong men who organized governments, built up vast commercial undertakings, created a civilization. Yet it was also a religion for the defeated and would-be defeated who retired from the struggles of life and sought a means of gaining postmortem bliss. From an unhistorical point of view such tendencies seem contradictory, most unlikely to be coöperative in the development of the idea of God. Yet coöperate they did. Their method of coöperation is like that of the Hebrew and Hellenistic elements in bringing about the doctrine of the Trinity. Those who represented the two estimates of life were members of the same social group, the church. Within that group asceticism and the social process were combined. The resulting idea of God was a scholastic legitimatization of the conceptions of God which had become dominant in the actual behavior of the Christian group which prepared for heaven by penance and founded a civilization by war and trade.

To understand the development of Western Christianity one must realize that Christian beliefs were constantly being transformed into decisions which had the nature of law. Unity in the church, like the unity of the Roman Empire, was dependent upon law. Freedom of speculation was not possessed by a group under authority. The development of the idea of God was always subject to the control of the church which in turn was controlled by the authority of previous councils and the belief in its own supernatural authority in all aspects of life. The elemental acts of life became sacraments. When one takes into account the intellectual poverty of the Western world from the fifth to the eleventh centuries, it is not surprising that authoritative formulas as to God became increasingly assured and decreasingly philosophical.

Lack of democracy and of scientific training always tends to insistence upon doctrinal regularity. Questions which arise from what might be called a lay interpretation of the Scripture are not so easily answered by argument as by the expression of authority. The early centuries of the Middle Ages were by no means uninterested in the profound questions of theology, but discussion was not permitted to form independent groups of Christians. The adoptionist heresy which attempted to give a Christology more in accordance with the synoptists than the Hellenistic metaphysics was crushed by authority rather than by argument. Other attempts on the part of imperfectly trained ecclesiastics to reëxplain the positions of the church were similarly treated. Disregard of the decisions as to God made by a supernaturally empowered church were treated in the same way as disloyalty to sovereign or to state. To protect the orthodox faith, the seventh century organized the so-called Athanasian creed in which salvation is declared to depend upon the acceptance of the correct doctrine of God. This doctrine is then set forth in easily remembered sentences which express the doctrine of the Trinity as it would appear to an unphilosophical, but thoroughly orthodox church.

This appeal to authority was more than a matter of doctrine. While the theology of the Eastern church used

the patterns of a prescientific biology, and looked for the
resurrection of the flesh, that of the Western church used
those of the state. In consequence Western Christianity
became transcendentalized politics. Rome had found
Gaul hardly removed from savagery and had built cities,
established great public works, introduced education, in a
word, had created a social order. Imperial conceptions
were as much a part of the historical process in Western
Europe as democracy is in the development of the United
States. The administrative divisions of the church were
those of the Roman state, the statutes of the Empire were
the model of church law, orthodoxy became identified
with group loyalty, and creeds and decisions of the Councils had the sanction of force as well as of accepted truth.
The Bishop of Rome began to be the emperor of a
spiritual realm.

How far this development might have gone had the
Roman Empire itself continued, one can only speculate,
for Western Europe met catastrophe. Its civilization collapsed. Its population was replaced by barbarians from
the North, to whom the rich cities of France and Italy
were loot. First as raiders and then as armed settlers, these
northern peoples destroyed the work of centuries and
settled down to enjoy the fruits of their conquest. Cities,
education, even literacy, all but disappeared, laws were
forgotten, society became composed of serfs working for
armed bandits who gradually gained respectability as lords
and vassals.

It is little wonder that in the centuries of catastrophe
that followed the sacking of Rome itself by the Goths,
human nature seemed to be worthless and men's achieve-
ments momentary. God and the world stood over against
each other in a dualism that was as practical as philo-

sophical. Then it was that Augustine laid down the base line of Roman Catholic and Protestant orthodoxy, the total corruption of human nature. It is not necessary for us to trace the origin of this enormous pessimism. It is enough to say that it is the sort of conclusion one would expect from a teacher torn by struggles between a sex complex and the fear of divine retribution, and from people who saw calamity without and passion within, who possessed no knowledge of biology, and to whom the Bible was a book of divine oracles rather than a record of experiences. At all events, Augustine believed, and orthodox theologians since his day have believed, that because of Adam's sin every person who had ever been born had been born damned, with wills responsive to motives which could spring only from a corrupt nature, destined to eternal suffering from which men had no ability to free themselves, however earnestly they desired or self-sacrificingly worked for salvation. As possessors of a human nature that had sinned in Adam they not only suffered the taint of blood afflicting rebels, but were participants in the guilt of that nature.

Over against this conclusion of a relentless but misinformed logic was the conviction that some men had been saved. Their corrupt nature had been regenerated and by virtue of the grace of God they were able to choose the right. But why one man should have this new ability and not another no one knew. Its explanation was hidden behind the veil of the will of a sovereign God.

Thus the concrete facts of human behavior, and participation in a political institution, gave rise to a conception of God differing from that which interested the theologians of the East. Although theologians and councils insisted upon belief in the Trinity as a condition of salvation, the working pattern of the West was a state in which a sovereign punished his rebel subjects and saved those whom he chose to save. Such a pattern in Roman thought was at least as old as the days of Cicero. Tertullian and Origen had long before Augustine spoke in general terms of the divine government, but with Augustine God's sovereignty was as central as that of the Emperor. Salvation was due to a sovereign's grace. But this grace was more than God's attitude toward those he chose. It was a mysterious power coming from God to the human soul. If the integrating pattern of theology was that of politics, the technique of piety was that of the mystery religions. The real fact was the organic relation of humanity with cosmic activities capable of personal response.

II

From the days of Augustine there were three chief aspects of the Christian idea of God: the metaphysical, which centered about the doctrine of the Trinity; the political, in which God was conceived of in the pattern of sovereignty; and the experimental, in which God's grace was brought to men through church practices. To these three might be added still a fourth, that of the mystic, which was expressed sometimes in terms which might have been used by one who had never heard of historical Christianity and sometimes in terms which identified Jesus with the object of the mystic's love. It would be difficult to find any theologian who succeeded in fully combining these four phases of Christian theism. Except when they are discussing the Trinity, the theologians of the Middle Ages spoke about God after the fashion of the Greek philosophers.

Thinking, however, was limited to the relatively small

group of those who had ecclesiastical authority or academic position. The lay thinker was relatively rare. Scientific thought included little more than what could be gained from Aristotle. Even that master was not read directly in Greek, but came to Europe through the Arabian and Jewish sources. The disorganized condition of Western Europe made any general intellectual life impossible. The experimental search for knowledge argued that a man had sold himself to the Devil. Yet almost sensationally, there appeared in the ninth century an Irish thinker who was a genuine man of learning and knew Greek—Erigena. He was intellectually self-reliant and not afraid to express his views, especially about God. Fortunately for him his contemporaries, although suspecting and disliking him, failed really to understand what he was saying. How otherwise could the early medieval ecclesiastics have endured such an aphorism as "Authority sometimes proceeds from reason, but reason never from authority?" As a good churchman Erigena recognized the supreme authority of the Scripture but he interpreted it as it had not been interpreted since Philo. A neo-Platonist, he made Christianity all but the support of pantheism, or at least of a monism in which nature and God, thought and being, coincided. The Hebrew idea of God was therefore merely a form behind which Erigena could see a God that could hardly be called personal but was the Ultimate Reality in whom all things inhered and in union with whom the soul found supreme bliss. Erigena, however, was unique in his independence. Modified neo-Platonism made no appeal to Schoolmen increasingly under the influence of Aristotle. To them the syllogism was more important than religious intuition.

The scholastic philosophy can hardly be appreciated except as one remembers that from the days of Charlemagne to the Renaissance it was endeavoring to reappropriate the heritage of unity which it had received from the Roman Empire. The complete disintegration of that Empire and the establishment of centers of rough and ready feudal order did not destroy the ideal of unity in organization and in thought. The church was the one institution in which this ideal continued. In consequence, for centuries religious thought was technical. In the field of politics the idea of unity found expression in the Holy Roman Empire in which Christ, as representative of God, delegated his earthly authority to the emperor and the pope. Naturally the pope claimed a precedence over the emperor. The struggle which ensued left in the minds of Western Europe a conception of imperial unity which in one form or another has constantly reasserted itself, sometimes with and sometimes without appeal to the divine will. Its most important and permanent residuum, however, was the papacy which in a striking way claimed to represent unity in Western civilization.

But enforced unity of organization under the guidance of God made the imperial office, with its authority unrestrained by constitutional limitations, the pattern in which Western theology set forth its conception of God. Such a view lies back of the discussion concerning predestination and free-will which since the days of Augustine has been in the forefront of the theological mind. How could a God have imperial supremacy and at the same time man have freedom? The answer, drawn from political and juridical practice, was, in effect, he could not in the major things of life, although in details which did not affect his destiny he did possess certain self-direction. Was not the citizen free to conduct his business even though he could not make laws for the Empire? In the nature of the case, therefore, man's best policy was to implore the mercy of God. In consequence the litanies and the theology of Western Europe centered around prayer for mercy, penitential discipline, and reliance upon the Son's intercession of the Father. Except for the mystic, God had retired behind the administration of justice and the exercise of grace. The Son gradually shared in this withdrawal of divinity and, like the Father, was to be approached through those who, like Mary and the saints, had a favored place in his regard.

The more the Roman Catholic Church reproduced administrative unity did it also demand theological unity. The papacy, like the ancient Empire, feared sects and felt it necessary either to crush them or, if it were possible, to absorb them. Imperial unity became thus the ideal for the Middle Ages, and furnished patterns and standards for every aspect of the religious life. God acted like an Emperor. His church was an Empire struggling with the Empire of Satan.

III

The same search for unity is to be seen in the effort of the Schoolmen to organize individual existences under universals or conceptions of genus by means of syllogisms. What the Emperor was as pattern to theology the "universal" was to thought. In it alone could unity be found. Notwithstanding opposition, Aristotle replaced Plato and logic, the beatific Vision. The "universal" is the original reality from which particulars come and within which they are contained. Reality varies with its approach to the universal. The ultimate and absolute universal is God. Theological thought required such a major premise.

Therefore the great question would be where it originated. There could be but one answer—in revelation. God thus became the assured antecedent to all thought. His existence was an *a priori* necessity which could not be proved by reason, but which could be made reasonable by syllogistic thought. Thus, while the operating religion of the church was developing rites, practices, the worship of saints and Mary, and creeds which could be used in liturgies, thinkers were struggling to show that, although beyond the discovery by reason, the truths of revelation were not hostile to reason.

The first outstanding representative of this movement was Anselm, Archbishop of Canterbury. He it was who developed the so-called ontological argument for the existence of God. The argument runs approximately like this: God is the most perfect being. But perfection must include existence. Therefore God must exist. Such an argument brought the immediate reply that while the idea of a perfect being must include existence, there was nothing to show that existence was the necessary correlate of an idea of existence. For example, a chimera, of which men have an idea, is known not to exist. In his reply Anselm modified his argument by saying that the idea of God was a necessary idea and therefore not to be compared with any other, for it is alone in its class.

Far more influential than this attempt to prove the existence of God metaphysically, was Anselm's presentation of God under the pattern of a feudal monarch. In the eleventh century feudalism was the most creative of social interests. By it the welter of European peoples was being brought into some sort of order. Notwithstanding the fact that the imperial idea still obtained, the landowning class, war, serfs, marriage, public order were all directly dependent upon feudal institutions. The controlling attitude which supported this social order was that of the scale of personal dependence of the inferior upon his superior. Feudalism could not exist in a land of equality. As one went up the scale of feudal lords from the knight to the king, there was a constant increase in honor. And this honor must be maintained at all costs, as otherwise the very structure of society would disintegrate. It was easy to associate this feudal conception of honor with the imperial sovereignty of God. This Anselm did in a little treatise intended to show why God became incarnate. The argument was not intended for those who accepted the fact of the incarnation on the basis of revelation, but for those enemies of the church who, like the Jews, Moslems, and pagans, did not admit such authority. The argument of Anselm may be briefly stated to be as follows: Man's disobedience had injured the infinite honor of God who was therefore under obligation to punish. He could forgive only when, in addition to the performance of the proper act of obedience, there was also something done which would satisfy his injured honor. Man must make this satisfaction if he were not to be punished. But that was impossible for a corrupt humanity. Therefore God in the second Person became incarnate, and as a God-man was able as God to raise to infinity the value of the satisfaction which as a man he rendered by freely dying sinless and without compulsion on the cross. God's injured honor thus being satisfied, he was free to elect some members of the human race to take the places made vacant by the defection of the fallen angels.

Such an argument would be quite impossible in a democracy or a constitutional monarchy. It is clearly the conception of a loving God in the feudal pattern. While it was not accepted by all of Anselm's contemporary Schoolmen, it none the less built itself into the structure of Christian theology so that to this day the idea of satisfaction of divine honor or justice is the basis of the doctrine of vicarious and substitutionary atonement. From Anselm's day theologians have preserved this feudal element in the idea of God. However he may have been moved by love to save a portion of mankind, he was not free to forgive until some of his other attributes had been satisfied.

The development of scholasticism from Anselm onward was not marked by any particular originality in the idea of God. Neither Pantheism nor neo-Platonism asserted itself even in the independent thought of Abelard. He might be able to find new analogies for the Trinity; he might even claim that reason could have given rise to the doctrine, but he never ceased to be a trinitarian. His great opponent, Bernard of Clairvaux, in addition to his all but unprecedented influence in the affairs of state, made one advance in the thought of God. In so doing he naturally thought in scholastic form. He argued vigorously that love was of the substance of God. That is, without it God would not be God. Despite the scholastic form of the answer, that which it set forth is of practical value. It amounts to this, that love is not an acquired quality of God. It is therefore not subordinate to justice or honor. It may even serve as an affirmative answer to the later question, Is the universe friendly?

The Jewish scholar, Maimonides, a contemporary of Anselm, was an important purveyor of the Aristotelian thought to the Christian church. How much Thomas Aquinas was dependent upon him and the Arabian interpreters of Aristotle, recent studies are making apparent. Maimonides attempted to make Aristotle a philosophical basis for Judaism. Long before Thomas Aquinas he asserted that there could be no conflict between the truths of nature and of religion. He set forth God in Aristotelian terms as the one who by his own nature must be self-existent, the First Mover of all activity, the logical *prius* of all existence. He was incorporeal, and yet could be conceived of by a rational anthropomorphism. Many of his Jewish contemporaries were not satisfied with Maimonides and regarded him as a rather dangerous innovator, especially when he brought his philosophical positions over into an interpretation of the biblical material and the rabbinical expositions. But Maimonides stands forth as one of the greatest of the medieval thinkers who gave not only to Judaism but indirectly to Christianity a philosophical basis for the God revealed in the Bible.

Thomas Aquinas, who had gained a knowledge of Aristotle through Jewish and Arabic sources, elevated the Philosopher to a position second only to revelation. For him there was a theology included in sacred doctrines, quite beyond the reach of philosophy. But the two were not inconsistent with each other. "Sacred doctrine is a science because it proceeds from principles established by the light of a higher power, namely, the science of God and the blessed." It derives its certitude from the light of divine knowledge which cannot be misled. It does not accept its principles from other sciences but immediately from God by revelation, and the subject-matter of this science is God. All things are to be treated under the "formality" of God because they are God himself or referred to God as their beginning and end. Theology cannot know in what the essence of God consists, yet the theologian can use the effects of his activity observed either in nature or in grace in place of a definition. Of course Aquinas held that a knowledge of the Trinity was given by revelation, but since the chief end of what he calls sacred doctrine is to touch the knowledge of God not only as he is in himself, but also as he is in the beginning of things and their last end, the problem of the existence of God must be answered first of all. And this he does in genuine Aristotelian fashion. He holds that the proposition "God exists" is of itself self-evident, for the predicate is the same as the subject because God is his own existence. Yet Thomas adds that we do not know the essence of God and so for us the proposition is not self-evident, but needs to be shown reasonable by such things as are more evident to us. In opposition to Anselm he held that to use the word God as signifying something than which nothing greater can be imagined does not establish the metaphysical existence of that which the word signifies, but only that it exists mentally. The establishment of the proof of the proposition that God exists lies in an *a priori* necessity of a First Cause or Mover and the necessity of the existence of something which has being of its own and does not receive it from some other existence. The order of the world would imply also that there must be some intelligent being who orders all nature in accord with a divine purpose. We cannot know what God is, but we can know what he is not, namely, he is not a body; he cannot be composed of matter and form, since he is pure act. As ultimate, he must be his own existence. His nature does not differ from his personality any more than his essence from his existence. He is therefore simple rather than composite. He must contain within himself the full perfection of being, otherwise he would not be

self-subsisting. He is not of the same genus as cr
although creatures are in some way like him.

When Thomas passes on to the consideration of h
lations with men, he finds a logical basis for the er
scheme of orthodoxy. Indeed, it might be fairly said t
the complete and firm union of Greek thought with Christian dogma was not reached until the scholastic philosophy had taken shape in the teaching of Thomas Aquinas.
Yet the formal language of scholasticism could not quench
his spiritual aspiration. To him religion was a means to
man's highest good. "The understanding is higher than
the will" except when the will "is set upon something
higher than understanding." "For perfect beatitude it is
necessary that the intellect should attain to the very essence of the first cause. And thus it will have its perfection through union with God as its object."

It is no cold intellectualism that breaks out from the
technical discussion of Thomas Aquinas as to "the sending of the Divine Person."

God is in all things by his essence, power, and
presence according to his one common mode as the
cause existing in the effects which participate in his
goodness. Above and beyond this common mode,
however, is one special mode belonging to the
rational nature wherein God is said to be present as
the object known is in the knower and the beloved
in the lover. And since the rational creature by its
own operation of knowledge and love attains to God
himself according to this special mode, God is said
not only to exist in the rational creature but also to
dwell therein as in his own temple. So no other effect
can be put down as the reason why the Divine Person

is in the rational creature in a new mode except sanctifying grace. Hence the Divine Person is sent and proceeds temporally only according to sanctifying grace.

Nor did the medieval mind limit its search for God either to logic or to the sacraments. There was the direct experience of the divine. As the Schoolmen sought to find unity by bringing details under universals, so the mystic sought to find unity between himself and his God in a Divine Vision. Syllogism and that vision complemented each other. Beyond the power of thought there was intuition which sprang from love. Sometimes this intimate experience of God would be gained by contemplation, sometimes by forms of discipline. But the common pattern in which it is conceived is that of the lover and his beloved, the bridegroom and the bride. While it is true that in many cases the search for the mystical experience of God carried men beyond the confines of mental health, it is also true that mysticism saved the medieval religion from being submerged in the Aristotelian rationalism. Neo-Platonism again stimulated religious experience. The mystical experience would naturally tend toward the pantheistic view as indeed it did in the case of Eckhart. But the Christian mystic was saved from pantheism by the doctrine of the Trinity. God dwelt in the human heart through knowledge and through love according to Hugo, but it was the Son rather than the Father to whom the mystic particularly looked. The Godhead in itself might be treated as impersonal but within it the three *personæ* could be treated personally. Thomas à Kempis was no pantheist, nor was Bernard of Clairvaux, who found in Jesus one who "healed men with example and strengthened men with aid." "I take example," he said, "from the man and draw aid from the Mighty One." In Francis of Assisi the union of the practical and the mystic is quite as remarkable. He found his chief joy in loving Christ and being loved by him. The abstract satisfactions of philosophy did not suffice for one who looked upon all things as sharing in the divine nature. "Praised be Thou, my Lord, with all thy creatures, especially milord brother sun that dawns and lightens us. He, beautiful and radiant with great splendor, signifies the Most High."

This faith in a God who could be immediately enjoyed by the human soul was the emancipating religious experience of the Middle Ages. There was no natural science to give unifying patterns to the soul who thought as an Aristotelian and loved as a Platonist. The God who had been revealed as the Trinity was known through the contemplation of his attributes or through fellowship with the incarnate Son as the giver of ineffable joy, moral ideals, and strength to meet the demands of each day. Thus theological thought was warmed by religious feeling, and religious feeling was checked and controlled by thought. Where scholasticism threatened to depersonalize the philosophical idea of God the love of the mystic kept his image very personal.

IV

By the end of the Middle Ages, the theological idea of God may be said to have been symmetrically organized. He is the supreme and infinite personal being, creator and ruler of the universe, holy, omnipresent, omnipotent, immutable, possessed of freewill, related to the world in the pattern of absolute sovereignty, predestinating men to salvation and reprobating others to punishment, pos-

sessed of a dignity that mankind must respect and forgiving only when satisfaction has been made it. Further,
this Being is portrayed in a high anthropomorphism, as
personally possessed of reason and purpose, approachable
by those who seek his favor to empower them for moral
living through his grace and the presence of the Son and
Spirit. No such conception of the deity had ever been
formed. It represents the confluence of the highest type
of religious thought and experience of both the Semitic
and the Aryan worlds. But such a God was the deity of
the theologians. For the unreflective masses the saints and
Mary were more approachable. God was a supreme sovereign with the qualities of earthly sovereigns raised to
infinity, though not possessed of any qualities which the
thinkers of the Middle Ages would regard as evil. Only
as we recognize that as in the case of Jahweh and the
Hebrews, the content of the divine morality was relative
to the social ideals and practices can we understand why
his representatives should have so unhesitatingly turned
to persecution and war as means of spreading the gospel
of love. So long as religion is a behavior dominated by a
sense of dependence upon supernatural power, it will be
conditioned by the morality of its adherents. And the
morality of the Middle Ages recognized no rights in
criminals and enemies.

This fact becomes dramatic in the acceptance of the
Devil as the chief torturer of the heavenly sovereign. As
the rulers of the Middle Ages had their torture chambers
and their force of torturers, so God had hell and the
Devil. Punishment was not inflicted on the dead by God.
He was judge and sovereign, but his rôle, like that of the
feudal lord, ended at the passing of the sentence. There-
after the sinful man, born already condemned for his

share in Adam's disobedience, was for eternity in the hands of ingenious and insatiable devils. It is not quite clear just where this terrible belief originated. Its most likely source seems to have been in the myths of Plato's *Republic* which found entrance into the Christian thought through the *Gospel of Peter* and then passed on into a theology conditioned by the brutality of the Dark Ages. Thus there grew up a dualism more concrete than that of Persia. God had no authority or at least no desire to exercise authority, if he had it, over Satan and his attendants. The saints might see from heaven the suffering of the damned, but there was nothing to be done in their behalf. They were under an irrevocable sentence of the infinite sovereign.

With such expectations of the future, it is little wonder that the Christianity of the Middle Ages, and later of the Reformation, should have been particularly concerned in salvation from the punishment in hell due mankind because of its participation in the sin of Adam and as a penalty for individual sin due to a corrupt human nature. Philosophical and theological ideas of God could have little influence in minds possessed of such a terrible apprehension.

It is from this point of view that we can appreciate the significance of what has been called a secondary Christianity, but which might more properly be called the working Christianity of the masses, both lay and clerical. To them Christianity became a means of avoiding the anger of a supernatural being through the church. Help both in obtaining divine mercy and for meeting life's needs was gained from personalities who by popular esteem and the decisions of the church councils had been given the position of saints. Masses who could neither read nor write could hardly be expected to follow the highly technical theology of the Schoolmen. It was enough for them to accept with "implicit faith" the decisions made by the councils expressing the will of God, and to follow such practices as made the contact with the supernatural world easy. Nor was this secondary Christianity without vestiges of an older polytheism. In Western Europe, as in the Hellenistic world, the Christian community had taken up into itself without any particular instruction thousands of converts from heathenism. The early converts were mostly adults, and they brought into the Christian church the ideas and practices which had constituted their religious behavior. At conversion they had disavowed Satan and all his works, and had renounced their heathen gods as gods. But they had not given up their practices and superstitions. The church to some extent met this situation by treating some of these abandoned gods and goddesses as devils and by appropriating the advantages that lay in the worship of other deities by making them into saints.

Thus Christian theism was supplemented by a naïve supernaturalism. In official Christianity we have the God of Thomas Aquinas, but in secondary Christianity we have a supernaturalism degenerating into superstition. Angels, saints, fairies, gnomes, elves, demons were closer to the masses than the God who was to judge the world at some future date. The repetition of prayers, confession, absolution and penance, votive offerings to saints and Mary, pilgrimages and crusades, the shortening of cleansing in purgatory by indulgences, all tended to separate human life from immediate contact with the God of the theologians. Indirectly these practices affected ecclesiastical monotheism, especially in that they served to elevate the powers of the church as the representative of God and of the priest who pronounced forgiveness in the name of God. Out from the religious behavior of the Middle Ages there was to emerge in the course of centuries such dogmas as transubstantiation, the immaculate conception of Mary, the infallibility of the pope speaking *ex cathedra,* which, while not affecting the official definition of God, were to develop a supernaturalism which was not born of the original theism of Christianity.

v

The change which came over Europe in the fourteenth and fifteenth centuries has generally been described as primarily that of an intellectual revival. Such a revival was undoubtedly present but it did not seriously affect the great masses of the people. The Renaissance at the start did not materially affect the God of the church. The hand of ecclesiastical authority was too heavy upon Western Europe to permit public discussion of its basic dogmas. But the new intellectual life of the fifteenth and sixteenth centuries was something more than a mere revival of Greek culture. The literature of Greece served to stimulate interest in fields other than those controlled by the church. Literature and art were no longer handmaidens of theology and worship, but existed in their own right. So far as religion went, the effect was not immediately perceived. So long as dogma was not questioned, it was possible to combine the new interests with the old, and religion and art were apparently to live on peaceably together. The frescoes of Michelangelo are evidence of how little the new intellectual life concerned itself with religion. Nor was the developing world of new interests concerned with the discussions of the Schoolmen. Scientists were not encouraged, it is true, and sometimes fell under the disfavor of the ecclesiastic authorities, but they aided in diverting the attention of thinking men and women from a happy life after death to the worth of life before death. In the earlier part of the Renaissance the zest for living quite obscured the fear of dying. Such an attitude conduced to conventional maintenance of religious practices and indifference to religious thought. The world was no longer a thing to be feared, but to be enjoyed. But to justify such enjoyment man must be felt to have worth in himself. A new mind-set was shaped which was not religious. The time was to come when this new sense of the worth of human nature was to turn upon religion and discover the weaknesses and inconsistencies of the church. But two centuries were to pass before the emancipation was attempted.

The idea of God, however, could not altogether avoid this attractive realism. Anthropomorphic conceptions were sharply confronted with cosmic thought. As men began to study the universe they saw it more as an expression of divine being than as something created once and for all by God. In place of logic came the beginnings of experimental observation. Instead of a God outside the universe we have a God working within it. "What is the world," asks Nicholas of Cusa, "other than the manifestation of the invisible God, and what is God other than the invisibility of the visible?" That was not the voice of scholasticism or of æsthetic realism. It was a promise of a new way of thinking of God. The unity and beauty of the natural world referred directly to him. The aspirations of the fifteenth and sixteenth centuries were no longer those even of Dante, but sprang from this new interpretation of the cosmos which much more resembles Epictetus and

Marcus Aurelius than Thomas Aquinas. God was to be known less by the aid of syllogisms than by mystical communion. Knowledge of nature was a knowledge of God. Fellowship with nature enabled the soul of man to participate in the Universal Soul.

If, through mysticism, theological thought avoided the neo-Platonic pantheism, the development of modern science was to carry the new view of God much farther. The development of the Copernican system of astronomy did not make toward mysticism but toward a cosmic God ever working rationally. In the teaching of Giordano Bruno, there is almost a prophecy of evolution. The universe no longer was bounded but was infinite. God pervaded all things. He could not be dissociated from natural phenomena. To study nature was therefore to study him. Compared with such a view of a God immanent in nature the transcendent God of the Schoolmen of the church seemed an abstract anthropomorphism. Nature was to be studied freely without any reference to God. The processes of human life were those of the universe and the material and the spiritual were really aspects of the same reality. Indeed, Bruno approached the Stoic thought of the seminal Logos in that he held that all things in nature are the expression of this inner reason and purpose. But Bruno was burned at the stake.

The full philosophical difficulties which lie in the conception of the divine immanence, men of the Renaissance did not perceive. Nor did they see that the development of an interest in a universe which had worth in itself was really introducing a rival to theology. The fact that the church struck out blindly against these early scientists, making some of them martyrs, was natural self-protection. A God who is reached by contemplation of nature and the human personality cannot be harmonized with the God of theology except by a frank recognition that theological concepts are of the nature of patterns. Until this fact is appreciated any line of thought, like that of Thomas Aquinas, a development of premises already believed, will see an enemy in any idea of God that has other origins. So it came to pass that from the Renaissance onward the increasingly emancipated intellect and the growing study of the material universe were phases of an independent movement at first professedly at one with current theism but later frankly its opponent. From the days of the Renaissance it may be said there were two lines of the development of the idea of God, the one within the limits of formal Christian religion, and the other outside the area of religion. The time was to come when these two streams of supreme human interest were to divide men into those who clung uncompromisingly to the idea of God developed by the Christian movement in its pre-scientific and scholastic stages, and others who found in the growing knowledge of the universe enrichment for the conception of God. The parallelism between this new differentiation of religious life and that of the early church is striking. As the Christian movement undertook at first to make the beliefs and practices of the Jewish Christians authoritative only to find itself taking over the philosophical and other elements of the contemporary culture of the Greco-Roman world, so the later orthodoxy of Western Christianity was slowly to find itself enriched by the concepts and methods derived from the scientists. Such a synthesis, however, was not possible until men had gained a new conception of the individual and organized new patterns for those persistent values which the ancient and the medieval world had expressed in pat-

terns drawn from their own social behavior and mind-
sets.

VI

The basis of the epoch-making changes that are called
the Reformation was economic as well as political. The
rural districts as well as the small nobility, the knights,
found themselves caught between two social tendencies.
Both were in large measure due to the modification of the
feudal system because of the Crusades and the disturbance
of the supply of labor due to the Black Death. On the
one side, there was the development of the upper feudal
class who were able to benefit by the changed social and
economic conditions, and on the other side was the development of the towns because of the new importance
of overseas and domestic commerce. As a consequence
the peasants both and the nights could not adjust themselves to the new situation. The peasants undertook by
revolt to gain justice from the nobles, but the small
knights found themselves threatened with poverty without
the peasants' recourse to revolt. The towns were to obtain
rights by war and bargaining with their feudal masters,
while the higher nobles in Germany found themselves
confronted by the effort of the Hapsburgs to maintain the
Empire. But all who felt the injustice and inequalities
of the new social conditions were at one in seeing in the
church a source of their troubles. For the church had
not only become the greatest landowner and financial
power of Europe, but its archbishops, bishops, and abbots
had become the uncompromising representatives of the
status quo.

In all periods of revolution, as in France and Russia,
or in periods of rapid social and economic change, as in

England, the church has been the most vulnerable object of attack. So it was in the fifteenth and sixteenth centuries. The intellectual movements of the Renaissance were less theologically constructive than disintegrating. A positive force lay in the rise of the modern nation through the triumph of great feudal houses in Spain, France, and England. Even where, as in Germany, this process of unification was incomplete, the desire for political self-control and that extension of law which brought the individual citizen, both municipal and rural, into contact with the supreme political power, whether king, duke, or ecclesiastic, led the restless new spirit of incipient nations to demand independence in the administration of their religious as well as their political affairs. Indeed, the Reformation might be described as the effort to express the new nationalism in all phases of social life. Men were not interested in religious liberty as such, but in a break from the control of the Empire and from the imperial church. Political ambition found in the religious revolt an occasion and a cause. For more than a century Europe was swept by wars in which the two interests were unfortunately so combined as to lay the foundation for religious hostility which has not yet been outgrown.

In those sections of Europe in which the matrix of law and politics was the old Roman Empire, these nationalist forces did not remake religion. The transcendentalized imperialism of the Roman Church with its accumulated attitudes and institutions triumphed. In the regions, however, on the flanks of the old imperialized territory many of the new states broke from the imperial church and set up state churches of their own.

This process had its inevitable effect on the conception of God. The doctrine of the Trinity persisted and to some extent likewise the technique of appropriating the grace of God through the sacraments, but in theology the pattern in which God was conceived became that of the absolute national sovereign, who issued decrees according to his own immutable will. With this divine sovereign, as with the earthly, the necessity of punishment was basic. Without power to force individuals to obey his law by punishment a king, whether earthly or heavenly, would have been impotent. This political pattern was used by both Lutheranism and Calvinism. The latter, organized by a lawyer, was a consistent extension of new monarchical concepts in the field of religion. The God of Protestantism was set forth in the pattern of a national king dealing with a hopelessly rebellious humanity, electing those whom he wished to save and leaving all others to the doom which was theirs because of their participation in the disobedience of Adam. The efficiency of such a view of God, derived from Paul through Augustine, is apparent to any student of the sixteenth and seventeenth centuries. It lies back not only of the organization of churches, but of the development of the American colonies and in the rise of the democracy of the eighteenth century. It was no form of defeatism, or compensation for human despair. Wherever the political and economic condition gave opportunity for the exercise of initiative, there emerged the paradox of the union of the democracy of the town meeting with the absolutism of theology. So long as there were unconstitutional sovereigns in Europe there was an unconstitutional sovereign God in heaven.

As a sovereign, God was under the obligation to punish all rebels, otherwise his sovereignty, like that of the contemporary kings in Europe, would suffer serious loss of prestige, if not, indeed, be ruined. This necessity to exercise his punitive justice, as it was called, gave rise to the belief that Jesus had borne the punishment as a substitute for the elect. Thus God's justice was satisfied and selected persons could be pardoned without threatening his sovereignty.

Two tendencies were followed by Protestant theologians in forming their doctrine of God. They varied in about the same proportion as the problems of politics were really in the forefront of consciousness. On the one hand, the Lutheran movement spread among peoples who were very little interested in reforming government and were content to accept the control of reigning houses, whether of royal or of ducal rank. There was in the Lutheran countries no outstandingly large city, and indeed, the attitude of Luther might be said to be that of a small-town man whenever he thought of cities and large commercial undertakings. Nor did he welcome the scientific teaching of Copernicus. The political patterns of Lutheran theology reproduced the undeveloped political life of the people. The control of the Lutheran churches soon passed to the state, and the clergy of necessity had little to do with the discussion of the politics of their patrons. The German states separated into warring groups, nominally along the lines of the religion of their rulers. Those who were loyal to the Empire remained Roman Catholics; others remained Protestant. For years the struggle continued between these two groups, expanding at last into a general European war, to which it seemed as if there would be no end. The Lutheran theologians, like the theologians of the Roman Empire, turned to theological discussion, but almost never to the problem of God. The chief issue in their discussion of faith and works was as to whether faith could be regarded as a work. One has only to read the

Formula of Concord to realize the immense care with which the Lutheran theologians discussed questions which did not affect their idea of God or their political status.

The other tendency sprang from the cities, and because of the name of him who became the first theological citizen of Europe, is commonly known as Calvinism. Here again one sees the share which political thought has had in the shaping of the idea of God. The central thought of Calvinism was the absolute sovereignty of God, who, as the Westminster Confession states, "hath all life, glory, goodness, blessedness in and of himself; and is alone in and unto himself all-sufficient, not standing in need of any creatures which he hath made, nor deriving any glory from them, but only manifesting his own glory, in, by, unto and upon them; he hath most sovereign dominion over them, to do by them, for them or upon them, whatsoever himself pleaseth." God's regulation of men was by decrees, and no small ingenuity was aroused, not to mention theological ill-will, by generations of theologians who were concerned as to whether the sovereign God decreed that men should fall and go to hell before he decreed that they should be created, or whether he decreed that they should be created and then decreed the punishment of the race which had fallen in accordance with his permission. Neither order of decree offered hope to the human race as a whole. Calvin followed Augustine more legalistically than did Luther in the matter of the original sin and total depravity. Out of the mass of rebels and corrupt and condemned humanity the sovereign for his own good pleasure had elected certain persons for salvation. The others he had not exactly reprobated for damnation, but they were damned by virtue of their descent from Adam, and consequently, strictly speaking, there was no need of election to punishment. That was accomplished by the decree already made. The election of those who were to be saved was a purely sovereign act. There was no reason for selection, for it had to be admitted that from the point of view of personal attitudes and habits certain of the apparently non-elect were quite as commendable as some of the elect. But a sovereign, whether he be divine or human, had no constitutional limitations. He elected whom he chose, and since he was God his act was good and beneficent.

Obviously the Calvinistic system is closely knit and logically impregnable. The one serious question that could be raised was as to whether the pattern of sovereignty was final. Contemporary politics, especially in England and Holland, tended to limit somewhat the absoluteness of the sovereign, and there appeared a group of very intelligent persons who attempted to modify the doctrine of the sovereignty of God. That is to say, they did not believe that men could be saved against their will, or that the atonement could be limited to the elect. From the point of view of our modern religious interests, these discussions between the Calvinists and the Arminians seem very remote, but in the seventeenth century the issue between them were as vivid and real as between Athanasius and Arius, Augustine and Pelagius, Luther and the Pope. The Synod of Dort in 1619 was the Calvinist Council of Nicæa, and shaped up a group of beliefs which put the final logical touch upon the theologians' conception of God. From that date onward, theological discussions have been either a liberalizing of the idea of divine absolutism or a frank abandonment of the pattern in which the belief in God was expressed.

We should hardly be justified in attempting to trace

these modifications in detail. It is enough to point out that for two hundred years at least they were largely within the political pattern. The father of international law, Grotius, contributed his conception that God's act of punishment was necessary for the sake of making plain that his act of love did not injure the existence of law as law. As a phase of the growing social philosophy, which was to find its classical expression in the works of Rousseau, many theologians came to think of God's relation to mankind in the form of covenants or contracts. Thus he made a covenant with Adam, which Adam promptly broke, and a covenant of grace which centered around the work of Christ. Humanity as it existed in the seventeenth century had no opportunity to choose between these covenants. It had all been done by Adam or Christ. The best men could do was to repent and trust that the sovereign God would elect them to enjoy the agreement made between him and Christ.

But God's sovereignty was not altogether unquestioned. The rise of parliamentary government, with the consequent deprivation of the sovereign of some of his powers was paralleled in English deism with the transfer of some of the powers of the sovereign God to nature. Scientific thought of the second half of the seventeenth century and the eighteenth century was very imperfect, but men were beginning to make a distinction between natural religion and revealed religion. In consequence among the educated classes there was a distinct lessening of religious fervor and a growing reliance upon a philosophy that, while hesitating to deny the ecclesiastical doctrines of God, was skeptical as to Christianity as a revealed religion. The behavior of the body politic was again affecting the behavior of men and women toward God. But deism is logically untenable. Men do not turn for help to a God whose sovereignty is limited. When this transcendental-ized constitutionalism passed over as a philosophy into France, it was foreign to the political behavior of that nation and in consequence became negative rather than constructive. The English philosophers were deists, but the French philosophers were atheists. The reason is ap-parent. The French had no political experience or organi-zation available for a theological pattern other than that of absolute monarchy. The church remained imperialistic among the Romance peoples, and any change in the con-ception of God, even though as in the case of the Jansen-ists, within the church itself, was suppressed.

VII

But other forces, not altogether recognized, were at work in the European life. The middle classes, especially in England, were coming into power. Both there and on the continent of Europe were groups who were not ready to accept the state as an arbiter of religious life, and who wished to worship God freely and, as it were, in a demo-cratic way. None of these groups, however, really modi-fied the current belief in the lost condition of humanity or in God as a divine savior. Yet the acid of democracy was eating into the aristocratic and absolute elements of theology. John Wesley preached the gospel to miners and organized a movement which in the course of a couple of centuries was to be powerful and widely extended. Little bodies of Brownists, Separatists, Anabaptists, Baptists, Congregationalists, endeavored to organize their religious life independently of the state. Their God was quite as awful a sovereign as the God of the Synod of Dort, but they were less inclined to be ecclesiastically subservient.

One striking fact, however, appeared in the latter days of Calvinism. The development of democracy at first sight seems to have had little or no effect upon the conception of God. In democracy, as in absolute monarchy, the concept of sovereignty was all-controlling. But while in the Reformation the pattern shifted from the conception of the Emperor to that of the national sovereign, no such change is evident in the rise of the *bourgeois* class. It might seem as if democracy had within it the possibility of stressing the immanence of God as distinct from his transcendence, for in the new political philosophy sovereignty lay in the people and it found expression in the government. Indeed, in the United States, where sovereignty found its expression in the judiciary, executive, and legislative branches of the government, one might almost say there was a potential pattern of the Trinity itself. But the creative power of political democracy seems to have expended itself in representative government. There does not seem to be any likelihood that democracy will furnish any distinct pattern for the idea of God. Republics are no longer greatly interested in their own political experiment. The creative forces of democracy are now economic rather than political.

This paradox in social evolution, however, is easily resolved when one recalls that it was the economic interests that really lay back of the rise of the third estate into political power. Both in the United States and in France the occasion of the triumphant revolt of the *bourgeoisie* was taxation and the problems of trade. Democracy was at basis a struggle between the wealth-producing classes and the surviving political authorities. In the United States this struggle by no means ended with the War of the Revolution, and our Constitution preserved the economic rivalries of different sections of the country. At the present time most of our constitutional questions have economic origin.

When one thus interprets the revolutionary movement which gave rise to modern democracies, the bearing of the forces which made the new epoch upon theology becomes clear. While the formal pattern of God remained that of a sovereign, his relations to humanity were increasingly thought of as those of a creditor to whom humanity owed a debt. The interplay of the political and economic ideas of God is to be seen in Jonathan Edwards, although that master theologian seems to have been unconscious of the passage of his thought from one pattern to the other. Evangelical theology combined the two conceptions of God's relation to humanity and in consequence there was an unnoticed change in the presentation of the doctrine of the atonement. Gradually but inevitably the economic pattern took the place of the political. With the new economic mind-set of the early years of our modern world God became a creditor who was under obligation to collect a debt from humanity. This debt was, it is true, still regarded as one of absolute obedience to the sovereign's law, but increasingly the vicarious work of Jesus was regarded as a paying of a debt rather than the endurance of a quantum of punishment. Evangelical theology has never lost this sovereign-creditor conception of God, and it is because of the insistence upon this attitude and quality of God that it finds itself seriously opposed by those philosophical and theological concepts which arise from habits of thought set not by politics or by commerce, but by natural and social sciences.

VIII

Until the middle of the nineteenth century, the only ecclesiastical groups that deliberately undertook to modify the orthodox belief in God were the Unitarians and the Universalists. The former refused to accept either the doctrine of the fall of man or the trinitarian view of the Godhead. They did not abandon the political pattern in their thought of God, but they did introduce into theological thought respect for natural law. In an age when democracy was accomplishing the independence of the United States of America and in France was denying the absolute sovereignty of the Bourbons, Unitarians set up the same rebellious, self-respecting attitudes in the presence of God. Humanity, in their belief, was not born damned but, certainly in New England, it was sufficiently respectable to demand its right from a sovereign God. Thus directly and indirectly Unitarians tended to break down the rigorous logic of Calvinism and to substitute for it an earnest philosophy of religion which, while claiming biblical basis and emphasizing the teaching of Jesus, refused pessimism as to humanity or the supremacy of punitive justice in God. In consequence they did not feel the need of Calvinism for the death of a divine savior, and the content of the idea of God was stripped of those subtle metaphysical distinctions which orthodoxy had erected into trinitarianism. God had duties as well as rights.

The Universalists were as logical as the Calvinists, but from a different major premise. They believed that love rather than punitive justice was the dominating element in God's character. He might be a king, but he was a beneficent king, forgiving rebels, and not content to leave any of his creation suffering eternal punishment because of the sin of Adam, or, for that matter, of any sin. It is true that the original belief in "death and glory" passed from the Universalist movement, but men of this type preferred to think of the reformation or even the final destruction of the wicked rather than their continued sufferings in hell. Sin could not be everlasting and divine love must be victorious.

The chief significance of the Universalists, as that of the Unitarians, was indirect rather than institutional. By the middle of the nineteenth century there is to be seen very widespread conviction that the fatherhood of God should be stressed. The atonement was treated as an expression of the love of God, and he became decreasingly an object to be feared. The revival movements which swept across the world in the last half of the nineteenth century decreasingly emphasized the punitive actions of God and increasingly appealed to his love and mercy. But the orthodox pattern of sovereign was maintained and the evangelical movement continued to utilize at least the skeleton of the conception of God which had reached its culmination in the Protestant Confessions of the seventeenth century. Orthodoxy was to a certain extent liberalized and romanticized, but structurally it remained unchanged. The God of the theologians was the God of the church. The Bible was the infallible basis on which to rest religious teaching and the work of Christ, as in the atonement, was an essential element in the work of salvation. Election was not stressed. The Calvinist system was treated with respect but liberally. Christian theism still included trinitarianism and the rubrics under which the relations of mankind to God were set forth were drawn from the political experience of the seventeenth century in which nationalist absolutism emerged as a factor in European politics.

IX

The second half of the nineteenth century saw a change in the presentation of God. Theology felt the humanitarian character of the social development and shared in an improved penology. While many of the preachers, especially the revivalists, held to the literal portrayal of physical suffering of the sinner after death, there was a widespread tendency on the part of the clergy to treat the biblical and even the ecclesiastical pictures of punishment after death as figures of speech. To be alone with their consciences, men were told, was punishment enough for them. At the same time, due to the weakening of the conception of political sovereignty, God was increasingly set forth as a Father anxious to forgive. The doctrinal definition of God given in the Westminster Catechism still prevailed—"a Spirit, infinite, eternal, and unchangeable in his being, wisdom, power, holiness, justice, goodness, and truth." It is hardly necessary to point out that in such a definition the psychological concept of spirit is undefined and has meaning only as long as the psychological concept itself exists. But the nineteenth century had no difficulty in using the term and attaching to it the beneficence expressed in the concept of Father. To antimetaphysical thinkers like the Ritschlians, God himself is beyond human knowledge but his love is revealed in Jesus Christ. Sin became ever more decreasingly dominant in religious thought and original sin through participation of universal human nature in the act of its first possessor, Adam, all but disappeared. In a word, orthodoxy was romanticized. It was inevitable that theistic thought should become confused. The social behavior and institutions which the past had unhesitatingly made a pattern for God and religion no longer existed or functioned ineffectively. In an age of transition no analogy or form of thought or social behavior was sufficiently widespread to take their place. The God of the theologian still existed but he was decreasingly a God of religious experience. The professions of faith in his existence were still made, but they no longer stirred the intelligent men to a fear of the wrath to come, or to a quieting assurance that the punishment which was properly due them at the hand of a God of justice had been transferred to another.

The God of the theologians, irreconcilably a trinity and a sovereign punitive and loving, jealous of his honor and justice but plenteous in mercy, is being subjected to as severe test as was ever Jahweh of the Hebrews. It is true that he has not been forced to appropriate the qualities of local deities. The stiff monotheism of the Catholic Church avoided any metaphysical polytheism by the simple method of letting dead saints attend to most of the local and personal needs of Christians. But the qualities of these saints have not been transferred to God. Their function seems rather that of intercession in the courts of heaven and in some cases working miracles in favorite localities. In popular religion, too, the God of the theologian has been assisted by miracle-working statues. In some groups the Christian religion has been a doctrinal monotheism and an operating polytheism. But such a description is only partially correct. The saints may have acquired power in heaven's affairs, but they were never regarded as divine. The theologians were so far successful. The use of images and the *hyperdulia* or utmost worship paid the Virgin Mary have never been confused in theological thought with the adoration due the deity. The Reformation eleminated these practices of Christians, but Protestant theologians, while holding true to monotheism, have very often made the Bible and orthodoxy the substitutes for the saints. Human thought about God is often remote from the practices of the religious life. A naïve pluralism seems more easily grasped than is philosophical and theological monotheism. It is easier for the mind to grasp the historical Jesus than the invisible God-substance existing in three *personæ,* one of whom Jesus incarnated. In the religion of worship and prayer men seldom distinguish between God and his *personæ.* Though in Catholic religion Jesus stands over against God, pleading for mercy, and God is urged by the litany and prayer to show mercy and vouchsafe to keep his people from sin, in evangelical Protestant theology, one distinguished theologian makes his test of orthodoxy, "Do we pray to Jesus? Is he our living Lord, omnipresent, omniscient, omnipotent?" Yet this distinguished theologian would have been the very last to say that he was polytheistic.

The God of the theologian has been assailed directly as either loving and impotent or cruel and omnipotent. Nor is it easy to avoid the antithesis. Any anthropomorphic conception of God, and above all that which conceives of him in political terms, is bound to suggest difficulties akin to those which would arise in corresponding human relations. Though the theologian would speak of his God as omnipotent, omnipresent, and omniscient, the human qualities which were thus expanded to infinity refused to abandon their grip on human thinking. In my opinion this antithesis was never entirely adjusted by the theologians. About the best they could do would be to take the position of Paul that the judge of all the world must do right. That which seemed evil must be either a discord to make harmony more perfect, or of the nature of discipline or punishment. It does not seem to me that such theodicy is very satisfactory, but probably it is as good as can be expected so long as the conception of the sovereign God of the theologians continues.

The God of the theologians met a new and vigorous opponent in the natural sciences. It was hardly credible that an omniscient God should have inspired the writers of an infallible book to record mistakes, therefore the Hebrew conceptions of the operations of God in the world were taken seriously. It is true that by the nineteenth century the theologians had ceased thinking of the world as flat, but they still pointed upwards as the direction in which lay heaven; they still believed that the sun once stood still, and that various miracles of the Old Testament were evidences of the existence of God. To doubt that Jonah was literally swallowed by a great fish was to doubt the deity of Jesus who in the gospels refers to that story. It is easy to see, therefore, why there should have grown up a conflict between the scientist and the theologian. The science of the Bible and the science of the laboratory and the observatory are quite beyond identification. Juggle with words and ideas though the more liberal theologians might, evolution was not compatible with the theological conception of God. To say that evolution was the way in which God worked was of course a compromise that helped souls in transition, but in it there was no solid ground on which a scientific mind could rest. Thus in the very nature of the case the theologian and the scientist lived each in his separate star.

But as a knowledge of the history of human thought would suggest, the logical outcome of these opposing ideas was seldom reached. So ingrained had the theological idea of God become in the Christian religion that any attempt to modify it seemed tantamount to atheism. Yet as the scientific habits of thought and points of view became generally accepted in educational circles religious souls experienced a sort of dissociated personality. In one set of relations they would be scientific and in another they would be theologically minded. The inconsistencies between the two mental views were admitted, but their solution was left to a sort of mystical faith which took both sets of beliefs as true without any attempt to harmonize them. In such a situation the God of the theologians was always forced to conduct a strategic retreat, and his surrender to the forces of culture seemed almost inevitable. Yet this defeat was only apparent. As Jahweh took over the powers of the baalim, the God of Christian theology is taking over the contributions of science. As the idea of God has grown in response to changed social conditions and modes of thought in the past, so is it growing now. Men still seek to satisfy the demands of a life process by getting some sort of personal relationship with those personality-producing and personally responsive activities of the environing universe with which they are of necessity in relation, but as in the past the conceptions by which such relationships are aided and rationalized will be organized at the tension points between inherited patterns and those drawn from the creative thought of the day. So long as this creative thought was political it furnished political patterns for religion. But now that the dominant interest of the world is scientific rather than political, economic rather than mystical, it must serve its religion with the patterns of its own devising. Where the tension is radical, as in Russia, religion will be treated as a vestige that intelligent people should destroy; where it is essentially autocratic, as in Fascism, the imperialistic religion of the Roman Catholic Church will be taken into partnership; but where a social order has been free to enrich its ideas of God from its own creative processes as in Western Europe and America, the normal course of a social psychology will be followed. The God of theology will be studied historically and the various conceptions of God will be seen to be patterns which help adjust men to the personality-evolving and personally responsive activities of their cosmic environment. The God of the scientifically minded will assume the patterns of science.

CHAPTER VII

NEW THEISTIC PATTERNS

THE God of the theologian has been the official God of the Western world. Millions of people have accepted him as he has been described and defined by councils and authoritative teachers. In countless churches they have prayed the Father for mercy, have eaten the flesh of the incarnate Son sacrificed at the altar, and have believed themselves possessed of the Holy Spirit. They have committed to memory definitions in catechisms and confessions, have discovered a plan of salvation by which the honor and justice of the Father could be satisfied by the suffering and death of the incarnate Son, have been regenerated and sanctified by the Spirit. They have trusted the Heavenly Father for aid and guidance. His will has been moral law and the Bible has been the revelation of the divine way of truth and life.

The God of the church has been very real—the center of a religion that has felt itself superior to philosophy, however much it commandeered the aid of the philosopher. But does He exist?

The historian of a religion is tempted to deal with its theological and philosophical aspects rather than with it as a form of human behavior, because it is easier to deal systematically with literature than with behavior. That is probably why the history of doctrines and religious philosophies so frequently seems abstract and remote from the religious life. But the idea of God can never be reached by any process of abstraction. To be understood, it must be seen as a motivating influence in human life. The God to whom men will not pray is only the ghost of God. A philosophy or ethics that does not lead men to pray is a denatured religion. Throughout the history we have been studying, it is evident that God is not a phase of merely philosophical interest. Men have looked for superhuman, cosmic assistance because they felt such aid was needed in their daily life. The God of the church has not been a doctrine of God but an inspiring personality. However explained religious experience is real. Theology has utilized philosophy to show the reasonableness of religion as a human activity, but its findings should never be mistaken for the God of Christianity. They are the accepted rationalizations of a socialized faith which seeks not a definition but personal relationship with cosmic activities on the part of the entire personality, with emotion and will quite as truly as the reason.

I

Yet it would not be far from the truth to say that religion has always been two-dimensional. In its upper levels its idea of God has tended to become increasingly like a mathematical symbol while in its lower reaches the practical need of divine assistance led men to turn to a supernaturalism always threatened by superstition. Men's religious fears are generally irrational and have been allayed by a secondary Christianity embodying survivals of primitive types of religious behavior. The difference between the God of Thomas Aquinas and the God of the illiterate peasant, however, was not so much a difference in recognized supremacy as in the way in which He was conceived. This secondary Christianity by virtue of its persistence and extent has been rationalized and given standing by ecclesiastical authority, but it does not affect the idea of God held by the theologian. The influences which affect what might be called the professional's idea of God come from quite other sources than magic or vestigial polytheism. Philosophy, physical, biological, and social sciences are creating new patterns. To men under the influence of these aspects of modern culture the God of the theologian seems akin to the gods of Olympus—an individual. They would say that they are religious but that they do not believe in God. So far as such antithesis has meaning, it would seem to be that men find themselves ready to accept the presence of reason in the universe, but are not ready to think of God in the patterns of sovereign or of spirit. To them personality means individuality, a quality in the deity quite incompatible with the demands of a universe in which galaxies of stars are grouped in super-galaxies. In other words, the patterns for the idea of God must change as our knowledge and experience expand. There is no difficulty in seeing that the political concept of sovereignty can no longer function as a final pattern for the deity. The universe is quite other than a state, and the relations of men to the ultimate forces in the universe are not those of subjects to an absolute monarch. In the very nature of the case, the pattern of sovereignty forces men to ascribe a personality to God which is of the nature of the personality of man. No matter how abstract is the portrayal of the divine sovereignty it can never escape the limits of individuality.

Similarly, in the case of the psychological pattern in which God is set forth as a spirit. Obviously this perpetuates an animism of which the modern psychology knows nothing. The concept of spirit has the advantage over the concept of sovereign in that it attempts to modify individuality in the interests of ubiquity. If there were any such entity as spirit in man, it might be possible to transfer it to the universe. This, of course, is just what has been done in current theism. God is immaterial substance which is coextensive with the universe but distinct from the forces of the universe in the same way as man's spirit was supposed to be distinct and detachable from his body. Here again, whether this spirit be regarded as immanent or transcendent, modern thought makes such a pattern ineffective. That there may appear a psychological pattern for the conception of God seems not unlikely, but it will not be drawn from an abandoned psychology. Indeed in many philosophies consciousness as described in psychological discussion is already in use as a concept expressing the self-directing, coördinating activity of the cosmos.

II

In the Illumination of the eighteenth century the spirit of the Renaissance was separated from the religion of the church. Philosophy grew rebellious. Inquisitive minds broke utterly with scholasticism and turned to nature. A germinant scientific method led men like Diderot and the Encyclopedists to philosophical positions in which religion was hostile to the contemporary religious thought. Some of them became out and out atheists; others, like Voltaire, satirical critics of ecclesiastical beliefs, believed that faith in God was necessary as a basis for public order. Spinoza's profoundly religious pantheism had left few traces on the eighteenth century theology, in large measure because of the rise of a new philosophy of human rights. Rights are a juridical rather than a metaphysical concept, and a thinker like Rousseau, whose mind was centered upon a social contract, could not avoid the conception of a Supreme Being who gave validity to the contract and justified men in the replevin of rights, which had been taken from society by kings and nobles. However much the eighteenth-century revolutionary thought might look back to states of nature and argue that the natural man had rights, the origin and pedigree of the philosophy of contract in the ecclesiastical polity of Hooker and the philosophy of Locke left a Supreme Being in control of the world. This Being was very different from the God of the theologian, but his relations to men were, like the Absolute of Plato, thought of in the pattern of sovereignty. The abortive and short-lived attempt of the Paris Commune to substitute the worship of Reason for religion was followed by the spectacular committal of the French Republic to a belief in the Supreme Being. Robespierre and the Committee of Public Safety were inspired by the desire to reincarnate the supposed virtues of the Roman Republic, and to free the Revolution from the antireligious excesses of Hébert, but they were not advocates of Christianity. In place of ecclesiastical rites there were symbolic acts signifying the dependence of men upon the Supreme Being in the conduct of nature and the revival of the virtues of the ancient world.

Such a political theism perished with the supremacy of Robespierre and left few traces in French politics or theology. It did, however, survive among the intelligentsia of the latter half of the eighteenth and the beginning of the nineteenth centuries. Ecclesiastical theism was in danger of being replaced by deism or so-called natural religion which had little use for the customs and teachings of Christianity, although, as in the case of Thomas Jefferson, it might turn with a sincere interest to the teaching of Jesus. Its conception of God was as far as possible depersonalized, and others than French republicans could speak of a Supreme Being and Reason without the acceptance of the theism of orthodoxy. Such a philosophical attitude tended to disintegrate conventional morality and respect for Christianity as a guide for life. But as is usual in such moments of reconstruction, religion reasserted itself. Although Bishop Butler's *Analogy of Religion Revealed in the Constitutional Course of Nature,* appeared in 1736, it remained for more than a century as an influential forerunner of the type of religious thought which seeks to utilize the findings of science as a basis for religious faith. In the nature of the case his argument was largely centered around design found in the analogy between the purposeful action of men as seen in their products and the evidence of a Creator as seen in the orderly course of nature. His argument was regarded by theists as final until the emergence of the theory of evolution in the middle of the nineteenth century. Even at the present time his general conception of analogy, as carried forward by Henry Drummond and others who are in touch with modern scientific thought, has its place in a world-view.

The attempt to conceive God as a personification of some permanent value in the universe is clearly an abandonment of the theological pattern. It is an intellectual interpretation of religion which is more akin to philosophy than to worship and prayer. It serves only to emphasize the chasm between popular religion and the religion of the intellectuals. It lacks, however, any pattern for establishing a relation between man and the cosmic activities.

It is a God to be thought about rather than to be lived with. Value, like being, is a symbolic term to juggle with when once it is used apart from human activity. But human values are set by conditions and limitations which are not to be discovered in the cosmos. At the best they are of the order of analogies. In the case of the philosopher, however, they are very apt to be of the order of mathematics, reached by the emptying of human value of all concrete content.

Such considerations as these emphasize the difference between the meaning of the word God in philosophy and in religion. The two will be independent until they are synthesized in some new pattern which will include within itself the element of social experience which is so obviously an element in the idea of God as the word has been used historically. It is characteristic of contemporary thought that new vocabularies and concepts promise the emergence of such a new pattern. But to-day, as in the past, an analogy will not become a pattern until by common use it gets to be regarded as something more than an analogy. And to-day, also, as in other times, the pattern must involve that which is unquestioned if it is to be really dominant in religious behavior. It must be as real to our modern world as sovereignty and spirit were to the earlier days. It must be as unquestioned as the conception of *personæ* was to the lawyer of the second century. It must be as much a source of comfort and moral endeavor as that of the God who imparted His grace and His spirit to those who partook of the sacrament and lost themselves in mystical experience.

Such operation of social psychology requires time. Its early expressions may very well be tentative, and its success be complete only when terms and formulas are automatically employed. A pattern is not a problem but an instrument of thought. So long as it is under criticism it has little emotional appeal, but when it is sufficiently in general use as to become a presupposition of thought, appeal to the imagination and control the expression of the entire personality, it will be the emotional equivalent of the patterns of earlier and less complicated social orders.

The process by which some new pattern for the idea of God is being tentatively and unconsciously shaped may be more or less distinctly seen in the field of sociology, science, and philosophy. In all three fields the God of the theologian is denied or ignored as no longer capable of answering the queries which arise from our social and intellectual situation. All these fields of intellectual interest are phases of that process of developing a type of thought which from the time of the Renaissance has diverged from ecclesiastical thought. Throughout this entire period, except in the case of those who were frankly defenders of Christian theism, the movement has been toward the dissolution of the patterns of theology and the substitution of concepts which were increasingly less individual.

III

The approach to the concept of God from the point of view of sociology is the least satisfactory of the three, largely because of its emphasis upon the phenomenal and disregard of the cosmic elements of religion. It is primarily historical and descriptive. The customs of primitive people are used to throw discredit upon the idea of God because of the incompleteness and unscientific quality of the primitive search for divine aid. As I trust has appeared in this discussion, such study is certainly legitimate as a phase of the study of social evolution. It is open to criticism, however, when it identifies the primitive ideas of an undifferentiated simple social life with the religious conditions and habits which have evolved as society itself has grown more complicated. To say that a modern man is not justified in holding to a belief in God because primitive man believed exclusively in fetishes, taboos, totems, personifications of natural forces, animism, and ancestor worship, is as illogical as to believe that a highly complicated government like that of the United States is to be disregarded because men once had a simple tribal organization. Origins may help us to understand, but they cannot exhaust the meaning of that which develops from them.

Revaluation of religion by those interested in the study of society is, however, by no means limited to the students of primitivity. Since the days of Comte there has been a tendency to personalize society itself and to make identification with social process a form of religion. So I interpret the movement which in our day reproduces the positivism of the nineteenth century and receives attention under its new title of humanism.

The representatives of this movement are not wholly agreed as to their philosophical position. On the part of some, humanism is a search after the good life without any reference to assistance from the universe. It is loyalty to human society, a scientific control of nature, and an effort so to organize life as to forward the satisfaction of human needs and enable humanity intelligently to face the storm and stress of human experience. The gods are, after all, only the formulation of imperfect human knowledge, and are not to be treated seriously. They have been born, have grown old, and have died. What is left are social values, social needs, scientific improvement. The call which this sort of humanism makes is noble and appealing, but in no strict sense of the word can it be called religious. As a system it stops at the point where religion in the historical sense of the word begins. And, therefore, it lacks a ground of faith and hope for its own idealism.

On the other hand, there are humanists who would not deny the presence of personality-producing forces within the universe, but they do not attempt to utilize them in the development of human satisfactions. They lay exclusive emphasis on the social demands of our life, and would be ready to say that, in a sense, these efforts are an attempt of men to make themselves at home in the universe. But they see no need of adapting any technique of gaining help from those personality-producing forces, the existence of which they admit. At the best men have a cosmic process without a God and the agony which comes from relationship with such a process is to be endured or mitigated by exclusively human means. Unlike the first group of humanists, they advance to the frontier of human experience, believe there is that which is beyond experience but that it is negligible in so far as human effort is concerned. God is to them an outgrown term the use of which would subject a humanist to misinterpretation as standing for a conception such as theological theism involves.

As regards the earnest effort to substitute human endeavor for human coöperation with the forces which have made humanity possible, it seems only fair to say that it must arouse a great deal of sympathy on the part of those who approach the problems of religion from the historical point of view. But if we are to make no postulate of metaphysical reality and are to ignore the effect of environment upon that which it has helped produce, humanism seems a confession of human defeat. From this point of view the efforts of the past to get help from what has been believed to be divine sources have collapsed and are unworthy of intelligent realists.

On the other hand, if humanism includes a conception of the total relationship in which men live, then it is capable of leading to something more definitely religious, and to a conception of God which, while not identical with historical theism, is none the less genuine and intellectually tenable. For it leads to the conception which will be later developed, that the universe is not to be relegated to a complete inactivity. So long as there is process, the operation of those personal forces which humanism recognizes in humanity are to be treated as continuing elements in the environment in which humanity develops. The direction of human evolution becomes a matter of technique, but not a matter of exclusively human accomplishment. For no matter how clearly the demands of social life may be emphasized, it is but one element of a situation, another element of which are those cosmic forces which have carried humanity to its powers of reasonable self-direction and continued as elements within the situation itself. A study of human behavior which attempts to coördinate itself with such continuing cosmic forces will serve as an approach, and it may be a technique for help-gaining adjustment with the forces themselves. The chief criticism, therefore, that I would place upon humanism is that it neglects elements of the actual situation in which evolution takes place. It studies the organism and its behavior, but neglects the environment upon which the organism has been and is still dependent. As someone has perti-

nently said, "It deals with a race of brothers as if they
never had a father."

Humanism resembles a more philosophical system
which has been set forth by a number of people who are
not ready to stop short of cosmic activity. Thus Mr. Wells
can speak of an ultimate, unfathomable mystery of the
universe with which humanity does not come into touch.
From this state of being proceeds, in a fashion which
resembles that described by Gnosticism, a Life Force
which is seen in all forms of living things. It is, however,
not God; it might better be called the impersonal Force
of nature corresponding to the demiurge of Gnosticism.
God in some mysterious way breaks into the confusion
made by this Life Force as a spirit who works in men
and through men. He is not omnipotent but is struggling
toward that which is better, and humanity must struggle.
This God can be known as he "stands close to our
inmost being, ready to receive us and to use us to
rescue us from the chagrins of egotism and take us into
his immortal adventure." But this adventure began with
humanity, and although Mr. Wells' combination of the
concept of process with that of divine Person is more
pictorial than precise, this God with whom we come into
contact personally hardly differs from the spirit of humanity itself. This identification of God with a personification of the whole of human experience is rather a favorite
with men who hesitate to think of God as either impersonal process or objectively personal. It is poetical rather
than metaphysical, including "the figure of myriad lives
and yet one vast group life in ceaseless activity." Its God,
in other words, is being evolved by humanity and growing
with society and the world.

IV

The scientific construction of an idea of God is as varied as the scientists who make the approach. Speaking somewhat generally, the scientist who has become a master of a particular field of observation and experiment is not accustomed to deal with his own findings in the spirit of the philosopher. When he comes to dealing with religion, he is apt to abandon his own method and to plunge either into a profession of personal faith which he has gained from his association with the church or to follow consistently his scientific method up to the confines of his science, and then plunge like a mystic into the unknown that lies before him.

Eddington distinctly repudiates determinism as at the basis of world structure. In his opinion, scientific investigation does not lead to knowledge of the intrinsic nature of things. Classical physics, he holds, forced a deterministic scheme on us by the trick of smuggling an unknown future that is dependent upon velocity which is known only after it is caused. Thus causality is dropped in the external world. It is physically improbable that each atom in the brain has its duty so precisely allotted that the control of its behavior would prevail over all other possible irregularities of all the other atoms. The mind has power not only to decide the behavior of atoms individually, but to affect systematically large groups. Indeed, he argues that the indeterminacy recognized in the modern *quantum* theory is only a partial step toward freeing our actions from deterministic control. Even statistical results are therefore not final. The materialist is forced not only to "translate into material configurations multifarious thoughts and images of the mind, but must surely not neglect to find some sort of physical substitute for the ego."

At this point he plunges into his mysticism. "The familiar material world of everyday conception, though lacking somewhat in scientific truth, is good enough to live in; it is a symbolic world and the one thing that could live comfortably in it would be a symbol, but I am not a symbol; I am compounded of that mental activity which is from the non-mystical points of view a nest of illusion. The mystic's conception of his spiritual environment is not to be compared with the scientific world pointer readings; it is an everyday world to be compared with the formal world of experience; it is no more real and no less real than that. It is not a world to be analyzed, but a world to be lived in. Because we are unable to render exact account of our environment it does not follow that it would be better to pretend that we live in a vacuum. The problem of the scientific world is therefore a part of a broader problem, the problem of all experience. The physical world is entirely abstract and without actuality apart from its linkage to consciousness.

Eddington repudiates the attempt to prove the distinctive beliefs of religion either from the data of physical science or by the method of physical science. The postulate of a mystical religion he bases not on science, but on a self-known experience truly fundamental. Certain states of consciousness have at least equal significance with those which are called sensations. We have to build a special world out of symbols taken from our own personality, as we build a scientific world out of the symbols of the mathematician. We must be able to approach the World Spirit in the midst of our cares and duties in that simpler relation of spirit to spirit in which all true religion finds expression. The idea of a universal mind or Logos would be, he thinks, a fairly plausible inference from the present state of scientific theory; at least it is in harmony with it, but if so, all that our inquiry justifies us in asserting is a pure colorless pantheism. Science cannot tell whether the World Spirit is good or evil, and its halting argument for the existence of a God might equally well be turned into an argument for the existence of a devil. Since physical science has limited its scope so as to leave a background which we are at liberty to, or even invited to, fill with a reality of special import, we have yet to face the most difficult criticism from science, namely, have we any reason to regard the religious interpretation currently given to it as anything more than muddle-headed romancing? In a word, therefore, Eddington holds that there are two domains of reality, one handled by science and the other by religion. The realm of religious experience is as real as that of natural science.

Jeans and Millikan similarly would separate the field of science from that of religion, holding that each is legitimatized by experience.

Morgan in his volume, *Emergent Evolution,* says: "I acknowledge a physical world which I admit is not proved. I acknowledge also God, who is, I contend, not disproved. And, so far as I can judge, both acknowledgements work." More definitely Thomson holds that Nature is congruent with a religious interpretation partly because of "the scientific disclosure of order, unity, simplicity, and advance, partly because of the cumulative suggestion that Nature is Nature with a purpose, partly because there are discernible in Nature certain great trends which are in the direction of what man at his best has regarded as Progress." Personally Thomson leans to a panpsychism because there is nothing inanimate. By this he means that all creation has a metakinetic aspect, the analogue of the mind of man and of all the more effective animals.

This conclusion, however, is not drawn by Sellars from approximately the same premises.

In his *Substance of Faith* Sir Oliver Lodge says:

> It is sometimes said that the operations of nature are spontaneous; and that is exactly what they are. That is the meaning of immanence. "Spontaneous," used in this sense, does not mean random and purposeless and undetermined; it means actuated and controlled from within, by something indwelling and all pervading and not absent anywhere. The intelligence which guides things is not something external to the scheme, clumsily interfering with it by muscular action, as we are constrained to do when we interfere at all; but is something within and inseparable from it, as human thought is within and inseparable from the action of our brains.
>
> In some partially similar way we conceive that the multifarious processes in nature, with neither the origin or maintenance of which have we had anything to do, must be guided and controlled by some Thought and Purpose, immanent in everything, but revealed only to those with sufficiently awakened perceptions. . . . The idea that the world as we know it arose by chance and fortuitous concourse of atoms is one that no science really sustains, though such an idea is the superficial outcome of an incipient recognition of the uniformity of nature—a sequel to the perception that there is no capricious or spasmodic interference with the course of events and no changes

of purpose observable therein—such as we are accustomed to in works of human ingenuity and skill.

Julian S. Huxley sees the so-called conflict between religion and science to be really between science and theologies. Religion, he holds, cannot be destroyed because "the religious spirit is just as much a property of human nature as the scientific spirit." Both have their parts to play in the experiment of human living. "Both can join hands in the great experiment of man insuring that men shall have life and have it more abundantly."

Such views of scientists should not be regarded as those uniformly held. They are, however, representative of a growing tendency to answer the questions raised by religion without recourse to theology.

v

An outstanding characteristic of the modern philosophical construction of the idea of God is that it makes our scientific knowledge a point of departure. This, of course, is inevitable, because in our present conception of nature and of man it would be quite impossible to proceed after the manner of Plato, with a sharp dualism between the world of ideas and the world of sense. Probably the two philosophical approaches most characteristic of our time would be roughly that through the conception of values and an evolutionary process which often presupposes a metaphysical monism.

On the side of the philosophy of values, there is the undeniable assertion that men are not content simply with a description of existence, but seek that which is of real meaning in their own lives. That is to say, religion is in a way selective, whatever may be one's metaphysics as to

the ultimate nature of reality. The philosophy of Höff-
ding, that religion is a search for ultimate and permanent
values, must lead even the most abstract thinker into the
realm of personality. The universe which in human relations is productive of values, whatever its ultimate nature
may be, is the correlate of the human search for values.
But in the nature of the case, the thoroughgoing pragmatist would stop at this point, refusing to commit himself
to any description of existential infinity. This gives rise
to the idea of a finite God in the case of H. G. Wells and
Rashdall, and in other cases to a pluralistic system like
that of James. But it is quite impossible to think that
value is not in some way the obverse of being. In any
case the world of values, although it be not that of Plato
or Eucken, is sufficient to end a materialistic or mechanistic
world-view. For if there be any trend in humanity toward
the organization of ultimate values, the step to some type
of belief in God is inevitable just as soon as one has the
courage to make it tentatively.

And the same thing is to some extent true from the
point of view of monism. If one makes the postulate of
an original single activity, an empirical knowledge of the
world in which we live makes it plain that this activity
has had the power of combination and recombination to
the point where humanity emerges. This might lead to a
new type of pantheism, but not necessarily, if one approaches metaphysics with a recognition of value-producing forces. What one would then have would be two
lines of evolution, one stopping short with the animal and
the other moving on to that which is personal. No strict
teleology would be necessary, tendencies would be undeniable. The organization of the actual facts given by the
science would indicate the emergence of characteristics

potential in the original activity which, in the nature of the case, can be thought of only as infinite, though knowable as its various expressions are conditioned by human experience.

Current philosophy is by no means uniformly theistic. Russell, Smuts, Sellars, M. C. Otto represent divergent theories that are at one in not affirming to theistic faith. Our task, however, is not to give an encyclopædic account of various systems but to discover how representative philosophers go about their construction of an idea of God.

The terminology of the metaphysics of Whitehead renders it obscure, but its religious conclusions are fairly clear. It does not champion either panpsychism or monism. Yet it is not the enemy of either. Whitehead enters the realm of philosophy as a mathematician and physicist. To him God is the "Principle of Concretion." By this he means that everything that exists implies the existence of all being. Thus a flower is the outcome of the totality of the cosmic forces, and around it all that ever was or is or will be may be arranged in concentric circles. The flower "prehends" all being, the universe "concreted" the flower. But the flower would not be possible without the infinite number of existences. Mathematical forms have reality. There are different levels in the prehension of the universe according to the extent of such prehension. But the many is always being concreted into one in accordance with these forms. And this is due to the nature of being itself. God is this inherent nature of all being. There is an actual world because there is an order in nature. This order is æsthetic and is derived from the immanence of God. The æsthetic order includes the moral. Whitehead avoids pantheism by representing God as order, opposed to the tendency to disorder and transcending the world of actuality.

In his *Process and Reality,* Whitehead attempts to carry his philosophy into the region of theism. Thus he says, "In the first place, God is not to be treated as an exception to all metaphysical principles, invoked to save their collapse. He is their chief exemplification.

"Viewed as primordial, he is the unlimited conceptual realization of the absolute wealth of potentiality. In this aspect, he is not before all creation, but *with* all creation." . . . "But God, as well as being primordial, is also consequent. He is the beginning and the end. He is not the beginning in the sense of being in the past of all members. He is the presupposed actuality of conceptual operation, in unison of becoming with every other creative act. Thus by reason of the relativity of all things, there is a reaction of the world on God. The completion of God's nature into a fullness of physical feeling is derived from the objectification of the world in God. He shares with every new creation its actual world; and the concrescent creature is objectified in God as a novel element in God's objectification of that actual world."

He then goes on to say, in the spirit of the theist, "The image—and it is but an image—the image under which this operative growth of God's nature is best conceived, is that of a tender care that nothing be lost. The consequent nature of God is his judgment on the world. He saves the world as it passes into the immediacy of his own life. It is the judgment of a tenderness which loses nothing that can be saved. It is also the judgment of a wisdom which uses what in the temporal world is mere wreckage.

"Another image which is also required to understand his consequent nature, is that of his infinite patience."

Pringle-Pattison holds that "man is organic to nature and that nature is organic to man." He thinks of God as no "Absolute existing in solitary bliss and perfection, but a God who lives in the perpetual giving of himself, who shares the life of his finite creatures," who is "the eternal Redeemer of the world." God exists as a self-communicating life. "In theological language creation is an eternal act of process—which must be ultimately understood not as the making of something out of nothing but as the self-revelation of the divine in and to finite spirits." Such a view of course approaches the view that a cosmic self-consciousness or the Absolute finds expression in centers of finite consciousness, but this is not Pringle-Pattison's conception of the divine consciousness. He would hold neither to pantheism nor panpsychism. For while the human consciousness is the outcome of the universe, it is objective to the cosmic consciousness.

James, with no sympathy with pantheism or the Absolute, declares "the drift of all the evidence we have seems to me to sweep us very strongly toward the belief in some form of superhuman life with which we may, unknown to ourselves, be co-conscious." But he cannot adjust this belief with any monistic metaphysics, and so holds that it is necessary to be "frankly pluralistic and assume that the superhuman consciousness, however vast it may be, has itself an external environment and consequently is finite."

As opposed to those who, like Bertrand Russell, would hold that process is impersonal and that a conception of God is not necessary, are those who, like Butler, would portray the objective world through a study of organic life. Each cell, while material, is also possessed of some sort of cosmic life which includes an organism possessing a larger life, and these organisms combine into the con-

ception of an all-inclusive Person or God. The consciousness of this Being must therefore transcend that of the
human organism, as that transcends the consciousness of
a single cell. Such a view of God is distinguished from
pantheism because its ultimate is personal, but it suggests
a still more ultimate combination of combinations, beyond
our experience.

Professor Royce, in his *Philosophy of Loyalty,* holds
that "the truth contained in the higher ethical religions
consists in the following facts: First, the rational unity
and goodness of the world-life; next, its true but invisible
nearness to us, despite our ignorance; further, its fulness
of meaning despite our barrenness of present experience;
and yet more, its interest in our personal destiny as moral
beings; and finally, the certainty that, through our actual
human loyalty, we come, like Moses, face to face with the
true will of the world, as a man speaks to his friend."

VI

It is plain that such views as these abandon the patterns
in which the deity is set forth by the Christian theology.
Sovereignty and even paternity are too anthropomorphic
to fit with our increasing knowledge of the universe. The
patterns which now must be used are not derived from
politics but from science. We are thus carrying forward
the process which has been traced. As men's knowledge
of their surroundings increased, the idea of God grew also.
Gods who have been outgrown have been discarded or
demoted. The gods that grew were those regarded as
capable of helping men meet tensions set by new knowledge or new social conditions, and were described in patterns which included the new conditions. A god of a
tribe was like a tribal chieftain; the god of an empire was

like an emperor; and now the God of the universe in space-time must be conceived of as activity that is both creative and environing. That is to say, the pattern must involve the conception of process which now dominates our scientific thought. But it is just here that we find the old struggle reëmerging between the patterns that include and those that exclude human personality. If our conception of the cosmic process is limited to the pattern of the apparatus of scientific study or the machines with which we utilize the forces of nature, the word God will have to be used in an entirely new sense. The personal element in the world is persistent in its usage. The conception of principle is only a variant of that of process and carries with it no personal connotation. One cannot speak of a principle as God.

But we face something much more than a war between terms. The vital issue is whether the universe in which we live as persons has any power to produce us as persons. If, as we must say, in the light of science, a negative answer is logically absurd, the pattern with which we describe our relations with a cosmic ultimate must include our experience as living persons. Only thus can a cosmic ultimate be conceived of as environing personalities and becoming an element in a dynamic situation in which such personalities are also elements. As the organism is in the environment, as the individual responds to the mind-sets of the group to which he belongs, so men are at one with the personality evolving activities of the universe. To-day as always, a religion is the adjustment of the entire person, however it may be described, to its environment. Primarily it is emotional and vital, and only defensively is it rational. We cannot escape the imperatives of the urge of life, but neither can we escape the desire to legitimatize and direct our religious life by showing how coherent it is with the whole range of experience and knowledge. The rise of new patterns by which we express the relations of ourselves to the cosmos and of cosmic activity to us as conscious organisms will be a new impulse to a sane and enriched religious experience. As has already been said, patterns are instrumental. Ideas of God help give content and direction to religious behavior.

VII

To discover the actual values which are set forth in the patterns by which men have expressed their growing idea of God, we must regard them as analogies. The most persistent of these analogies are the relation of the ruler to his subjects. When interpreted, they are seen to express the following convictions:

1. Mankind is dependent on superhuman powers or beings in the universe.

2. These powers or beings, if treated in the same way as our human authorities, can be made propitious and helpful.

3. Religion is thus an extension of personal life into relations with superhuman power and being.

4. This adjustment is aided by a personal conception of the powers or beings.

5. Morality is obedience to the will of this person.

Obviously such values do not utilize our present knowledge of the universe. They are all prescientific in origin. If religious behavior and belief in God are to continue in a world dominated by scientific methods of thought, a pattern must be found which will express the equivalents of these earlier values. These may be restated thus:

1. The universe is not mechanistic, but capable of

evolving human persons and of furnishing an environment in which their personality can be preserved and furthered. The activities postulated by such an evolution are constituents of the environment upon which persons are dependent. To seek personal adjustment with these environing activities is an expression of the urge of life itself.

2. With this environment persons can coöperate to form a dynamic situation which postulates mutual reaction between its elements. Such a situation is organic rather than political. From it we gain help in our personal development.

3. The experience and technique gained by living with human persons can be used for setting up this dynamic help-gaining adjustment with cosmic activities.

4. Such personal adjustment is conditioned upon conceiving the personality-producing and personality conditioning activities in a personal pattern.

5. Morality is both an action in accordance with and an aid to personal adjustment with the personality-producing activities of the universe thus conceived.

Can such equivalents of historic theism be re-expressed in an idea of God consonant with today's world-view?

CHAPTER VIII

A CONTEMPORARY GOD

THE historically minded person sees that all the various conceptions of the object of worship which we have considered are relative to the conscious needs and the dominant social mind-sets of various times and civilizations. The meaning of the word God is found in the history of its usage in religious behavior.

I

The patterns in which men's ideas of God have been set forth have been used as if they represented some objective reality. In the less critical times doubtless the worshiper thought that there was something physical exactly corresponding to his idea. The use of images and sacred objects is evidence of the desire on the part of the less developed civilizations to gain this assurance. As intellectual interests developed and men became more intelligent, the belief grew that any description of the deity was beyond the power of men. We have seen how, in the hands of the philosopher and theologian, the picturesque anthropomorphism of early days is replaced by the conception of pure being or by the anthropomorphism of prescientific psychology. Yet, whether the pattern used be that of king or of spirit, it was believed to represent an actually existent being. Even when the philosophical theologian arrived at the belief that God cannot be known in his essence, he held that the essence itself exists beyond the area of knowledge, revealed in its "effects" in nature or some individual.

This assumption of some existence corresponding to an idea is by no means limited to religion. Any pattern is likely to be treated metaphysically. Those who are accustomed to think scientifically are very likely to treat a term born of their experience as identical with that which it is used to describe. If one says that the electron is electricity, he is simply defining one unknown term by another that stands for observed activities, but the nature of which is quite unknown. Similarly the word life stands for a group of experiences by which we describe activities by which they have been evoked. To say that a plant is alive is to say that there are observed phenomena which are like those to which the term life has already been applied. But the word life, like electricity, is really a symbol as lacking in definition as the x of the mathematician. Unlike the mathematical symbols, however, such ultimate words are believed to have existential correlates. For that reason successive changes in experience connoted by a term do not necessarily destroy the conviction that there is something actual which a pattern enables us to use. If, for instance, one were to compare the definitions of matter made a hundred years ago with those which are now the starting point of laboratory experiment, it would be at once seen that the patterns have markedly changed. But nobody would deny the reality of sense perception or would claim that its physical cause were non-existent.

To recognize that the element of experience in every definition is more than a mathematical symbol is to affirm some objective existence evoking the experience. The word sun, for instance, would not be given the same definition by a savage as is given by an astronomer. The North Star may connote to a child a very simple experience, but to the sailor it is a guide to sailing, and to the astrophysicist a very complicated chemical and physical object, so far away that light requires years to pass from it to the eye of the observer. But the physical objects that evoke the varied descriptions exist. Every reality in the field of knowledge includes something objective and something conceptual. A concept is thus instrumental as well as descriptive. To put it in simple mathematical phrase, if a were to stand for a concept and x for that by which it is occasioned, neither a nor x is a complete reality in experience. Reality could not be described as $a+x$, but as ax. If we consider realities which express situations and so include relations like the word friend, we cannot disregard either the human being or that personal relationship which enables us to form a concept of this being.

The history of the usage of the term God shows that it is not strictly metaphysical or ontological. There is no existence exactly corresponding to the patterns with which the deity has been conceived. There was no Jahweh on Mount Sinai and no Zeus on Mount Olympus. No more is the God of the theologian a metaphysical being. He, too, is reality conceived in patterns.

Is, then, atheism the unavoidable outcome of the history of the idea of God? So men say who misinterpret the real nature of the word. That their misinterpretation is not wholly their fault is undoubtedly true. The popular presentation of the Christian idea of God has been too often a mélange of biblical stories portraying God as if he were to be identified with the Jahweh of the Hebrews. But common sense, quite independent of historical study, came to the rescue of the Christian faith. Apologetics followed suit. The presentations of the God in the Old Testament were said to be not what God really is, but what the people of biblical times thought he was, and they were in part mistaken.

Such adjustment of theological theism to scholarship might be called semi-historical, but it is not altogether consistent with the use which the theologians have made of the Bible. More than that, the non-theological mind feels that theology claims to describe some being other than the picturesque portrayals of the ancient world. It is not difficult to see, therefore, why men should say they do not believe in God and yet claim to be religious. They do not think there is any actual personality corresponding to any idea of God which has yet been organized. In so doing they are undoubtedly correct. But they are mistaken when they think that God is to be rejected as an outmoded metaphysical term. The issue is not so simple as the aggressive atheist seems to think. As our study must have shown, the word God has always been a word expressing relations, though its content has been furnished by patterns. But only realities can be in relations.

II

The starting point for religion, as for any other form of behavior, is a relationship with the universe described by the scientist. No matter how self-centered or subjective a man may be, he cannot escape the forces in the midst of which he has to live. Those that are physical are easily discovered. Man lives under the pressure of the atmosphere; he is a peripatetic laboratory in which chemical elements are continually combining; he is subject to the laws of gravitation and to radioactive forces. The change of a few degrees in the heat of his environment means death. He lives on a planet from which he cannot stray ten miles and live.

But these are by no means all the cosmic relations which condition human life. Otherwise there would be no man to write about. At the best there would be only animals. But here man is. He is unlike any other chemical compound or organism, for he is capable of at least limited self-direction, of ordering life to distant ends, of generalized thought, and of the organization of social institutions, art, and morals. How can such an order of life be accounted for?

The answer is again, the universe. The mysterious process which we roughly call evolution brought man into being. But if that be the case, then there must be activities within the cosmos sufficient to account for the evolution of the human species with its personal qualities. There must be personality-evolving activities in the cosmos. Furthermore, these personality-evolving activities of the cosmos must continue as elements within the total environment in the midst of which men must live and to which they must be adjusted. Otherwise men, lacking the environmental elements which aided in their evolution, would perish. That is the law of life itself. Every organism needs the environment within which and because of which it has evolved. When a water-breathing animal becomes an air-breathing animal two conclusions are empirically sure: there was air to assure his new existence, and if he lives he must be breathing air. An animal that has become personal, if he is to live, must live personally, at one with the forces that wrought the change. We can no more escape the influence of these personality-evolving activities than we can escape the influence of those impersonal forces with which chemistry and physics deal.

Nor can we live impersonally with them. Life must be expressed at its highest function and in accord with the creative elements of the environment which made that high function possible. Religious behavior is the outcome of such necessity.

The attempt to utilize personal experience in making such adjustments effective is the function of every religion. The efficiency of a religion will be measured by the efficiency of its patterns to integrate human life with those elements of the known universe capable of satisfying personal needs. The patterns may change but the search for adjustment is as imperative as life itself. Only a mistaken reading of the facts can lead one to believe that such relationship has disappeared when a pattern proves ineffective. To realize that the traditional conception of God as sovereign or trinity is no longer tenable is not to say that the reciprocal relationship of men with the personality-producing activity of the universe is an end. It simply means that in religion, as in physics, we must adopt new patterns by which cosmic relations can be rationalized and better established.

In the present state of our knowledge of primordial activity it is impossible to distinguish sharply between its different elements. The old-time divisions which could be drawn between chemistry and physics no longer exist and the difference between inorganic and organic matter is also growing less distinct. Electricity, radioactivity, light, and heat cannot be detached either from each other or from their effects in such a way as to make them absolutely uncorrelated with each other. Space and time are being fused in the conception of space-time. Yet all these various elements of nature are distinguishable in their operation and effects. Whatever may be the origin of heat and electricity we have no hesitation in saying that the experience which comes from fire and the shock of electricity are due to forces the nature of which may be at least analogically described and distinguished.

The same general statements would hold in the case of other phenomena such as life and personality. Despite the controversy over whether there is a separate vital force, we know there is living matter and that its continued vitality is dependent upon distinguishable chemical and physical conditions. We should not argue that the universe is alive because there are living organisms within it, but the universe cannot be understood except as possessed of forces which produce and sustain living organisms. The universe without such capacity of producing living organisms would be a different universe from that which we really have. Similarly in the case of personality. The universe must be capable of producing that which it has produced. True, it does not follow inevitably that because the universe has produced personalities it is itself personal, but it does follow that it has within it activities which are capable of producing that which is personal. This axiomatic statement is supported by what we know of nature. It is not legitimate to extend the qualities of the human personality to the universe because human psychology is conditioned by certain distinct physical limitations which we cannot find in the universe. In the very nature of the case the activities of that which is infinite cannot be safely inferred from the activity of that which has definite limitations. But no more is it legitimate to say that the universe from which persons have evolved is like a machine. Our experience of machines or forces forbids any such conclusion. The very limitations which make them impersonal forbid their inclusion in a personal relation.

III

But we are not restricted to *a priori* evidence that there are cosmic activities with which persons can set up personal relations. There is the evidence of observation.

While straightforward thinking should make us hesitate to extend human values directly to the universe, it compels us to postulate in the primordial cosmic activity the capacity to make personal life possible, and therefore to see characteristics of the cosmos which differentiate it from the machine. These characteristics have been recognized ever since men began to think. Sometimes, as in the argument from design, they have been used for direct proof of the existence of God. At other times they have turned men toward pantheism or panpsychism. But as the discoveries of science they exist wholly apart from any metaphysical use to which they may be put. Briefly stated, they are:

1. The vanishing point of our knowledge of the universe is activity. This activity has various aspects, one of which is the tendency to evolve, and to coördinate particular activities.

2. This activity in its various expressions is intelligible. Natural law is the general description of the way cosmic forces act. Mathematics by symbols can work out relations which are found to be true when put to the empirical test. Such characteristics are obviously analogous to those of human reason. Even if there be an element of chance or a break in the causal chain, as some physicists declare, the resulting phenomena are themselves susceptible to tentative interpretation as similar to the conative powers of the mind.

3. Within this activity it is possible to discover and trace tendencies. It is, of course, true that it is beyond human power to discover why the universe is and what

as a whole it is about. We are not yet equipped to formulate a cosmic purpose. Dogmatism has no place in metaphysics. But within certain areas it is possible to discover process. The data of astronomy, geometry, biological sciences, sociology, psychology, put at our disposal facts which would argue a process in which various activities of the cosmos are so combined, recombined, coördinated, that one can speak with the biologist Mathews of the "road of evolution" as leading to personal individual life. But an observable process with discoverable tendency is analogous to the powers which in human persons we call purpose and choice.

4. This process also has a practical bearing upon the welfare of the persons it has evolved. One may well hesitate to extend to the cosmos values which are distinctly born of a finite humanity but certainly a process from which humanity has come cannot be regarded as unadapted to humanity. But even when caution bids us hesitate to speak of cosmic values or of the universe as possessing values in itself, or, much less, of speaking of its friendliness, we cannot ignore the fact that cosmic activity in its permutations does have significance as a continuum presupposed by and perceived in human experience. The more one limits the area to which the word value can be applied, the clearer it becomes that man is organic to the universe, and that the universe cannot be understood if humanity is abstracted from it, and the value-producing capacity of the cosmic activities in human relations is ignored.

IV

If we properly interpret the patterns in which the idea of God has been successively expressed, we see that they stand for conceptions of the personality-evolving and personally responsive activities of the universe upon which human beings depend. The word God stands for neither the concept alone nor the activities alone, any more than the word friend stands for a sentiment or a human body. It expresses a reality because it expresses and furthers the relation between existences.

The formula for God is ax rather than $a+x$. On the scientific postulate of evolution, the personality-producing activities in the universe are elements of our conditioning environment with which we come into personal relations. The word God, when judged by its historical use, is our conception and experience of such activities in human relations. To that extent, as we have seen, it must vary in content, being instrumental rather than exclusively ontological. In other words, it is a term expressing an experienced relationship with an objective environment, which is an element of a dynamic situation in which we are also elements. The metaphysician and the strict pragmatist both fail to give the correct definition to God for the reason that each omits the relationship between the element which the other describes. If the historical usage of the word means anything, the metaphysician with his Absolute has no more a God than the pragmatist with his personification of social values. The word God in its religious usage does not stand for Being or a principle of concretion. It is a concept evoked by an attempted relationship with a cosmic activity which is other than the human subject. It would be, therefore, incorrect to say that the word God to a primitive man or the Hebrew or the theologian stood for unreality. Whatever enters into relationship with men actually exists, and the concept by which the relation has a resulting experience is equally real.

The idea of God is the outcome of the effort which men have made by the use of personal experience to gain help from those elements of the environment upon which they feel themselves dependent, and with which they attempt personal relations as instinctively as they breathe or protect their life. Personal life is always engaged in a quest for helpful adjustments with forces other than itself, by which it can be preserved and bettered. Such a quest includes impersonal, biological adjustments, but just as inevitably it also includes the personal. The difference between such adjustments to the total environment is due to the different demands of the persons making the adjustment, and the elements with which adjustment is made. The concept God is one of its means. In the case of those who fail to distinguish between the form and the function of the idea of God, any change in patterns is apt to be destructive. Under such conditions some will not only reject the inherited ideas of God, but will question the worth of personal life. Over against the religious view of men's relations with the cosmos, they prefer impersonal interpretations, and in consequence life seems frustration leading to frustration. But such a negative attitude is both unnecessary and illogical. The dependence on cosmic activities is more than mechanistic and is not futile. Despite superstition and ignorance, human history without the adventure in the projection of personal experience into cosmic relations would never have been.

As the activity of living matter differs from that which is dead, so does the activity which we call human differ from that which is impersonal. Of that, despite the definitions of science which are only tentative, we have no empirical doubt. The integrating, coördinating, concreting activities of the universe find in human beings different expressions from those found in crystals and the forms of vegetable and animal life. Both the personal individual and societies of persons are dependent upon them. Even though the word personality may, like life itself, still lack definition, we can see the human individual grow more intelligent, more purposeful, and more devoted to non-physical values because of relations with others of its kind. Adjustments of such personalized individuals must be more than impersonal. That is why the abstract conceptions of the metaphysician have so little motive power. We feel more vitally than we think. Theologians and philosophers discuss the attributes and the substance of God, but they invariably express his relations to men in some pattern of social experience. Intellectual processes, abstract ideas, scientific knowledge affect such behavior and demand new patterns with which men can be adjusted to the cosmic environment. But men have yielded to the adjustment-seeking urge of their own personal nature and acted religiously. They have sought integrating organic adjustment with personality-producing activities. The conception of God has helped men to regard these adjustments as more than matters of speculation.

Society is included in this cosmic environment in which men live, but not as its substitute. The personalization of the individual is the outcome of his coördination and interrelation with other human individuals, but society itself is not apart from the cosmic order. It, too, is subject to the personality-producing activities of the universe as well as the impersonal influences of geography and physical forces. The growth of the idea of God is due to this man-made environment, subject to the influence of the cosmic. As a social order has developed, new personal needs have affected both society and the individual.

In meeting such needs we adjust society and ourselves organically to the cosmic personality-evolving activities expressed in the integrating process from which society results. Social relations are mediating disciplines for a bio-mystical adjustment with the cosmic activities themselves. Love is the social expression of cosmic coördination on the personal plane.

At this point theological theism must be abandoned and a new theism organized. Such adjustment is not with a super-individual. A man becomes more individual in personal relations, but the idea of God becomes less individual. The god of the primitive person is thoroughly individual. He can be pictured as imagined. But men came to think of God as universal. So God was thought of in the pattern of the spirit, which is an early attempt to rise above the concrete conceptions of individuality. But even if, in the case of the divine spirit, the limitations of time are removed, those of space are still unconsciously felt. When men now undertake to utilize this psychology of body and spirit in their thoughts of God, their knowledge of the universe is destructive. It is impossible to extend the concept of spirit into the universe when it no longer has a place in our psychology. In its place comes a new pattern which is personal without individuality.

v

Here we meet our basic problem. How is it possible to enter into personal relations with personality-producing activities which are not susceptible of individualization? The answer seems to lie first in a pattern drawn from a living organism. Men must live in dynamic relations with an environment capable of preserving and furthering such relations. If the urge for the preservation and the development of personal individuals demands adjustment to the environment of personality-producing activities of the universe on the personal plane, then those forces themselves must be conceived of as capable of personal response. Otherwise there could be no adjustment. Only persons enter into personal situations. Such a conception includes the extension of the individual's experience into relations with other individuals conceived of as capable of reciprocally extending their own experience into a situation embracing all those concerned. So long as the object is believed not to possess such capacity, the attempt to treat it on a personal plane is doomed to failure. We can as persons control a machine, but it cannot respond personally to our control.

The pattern of organism when used to express the idea of God must, therefore, include personal as well as biological elements. The organic relation is social. But such relations involve anthropomorphism. Our mutual personal adjustments are conditioned by picturing others as like ourselves as truly as by picturing ourselves like them. For example, there is nothing ontological corresponding to the full meaning of the word friend, but there are existences postulated in the image which friendly relations involve. The relationships are aided by an intellectual concept. If they are exceedingly emotional, the image is a poetical analogy which appeals to our emotions through the imagination. If, when these images and analogies become conventional they lose something of their power of emotional excitation, they yet remain as patterns which aid in the establishment of relations. They seem to have actual existences. But they disappear when subjected to severe analysis. Contrast, for example, the images with which the poet describes love with the explanations of the psychoanalyst. Indeed, the weakness of much of modern psychology seems to be that it is too absorbed in the study of the vital mechanism to appreciate the influence of social situations on the development of personality. Perhaps this is one reason why the behaviorist psychologist is so critical of the social psychologist. Yet the phenomena which each studies are real. If the human person is studied as a whole in his social relations, the inaccuracy of any analysis is at once apparent. You cannot understand a rose by describing its petals and sepals, its stamens, its pistils, and its ovary. No more can one understand what is personal by analyzing the individual into only his vital mechanisms or by studying only social responses. There is a third element in reality. The concept by which relations of persons are conceived is as real as the persons in the relationship, for it affects the relationship.

Some element of anthropomorphism is as psychologically inevitable in the word God as in the word friend. The sort of anthropomorphism will vary according to the cultural content of the religious person. The more naïve the psychology, the more individually will God be conceived. The more one is impressed with the vastness of the universe, the mystery of human consciousness, and the non-materiality of matter, the more will the conception of God be the personal responsiveness of postulated personality-producing activities. For by personal we here mean "of the order of human beings in their personal interrelations, rather than that of principle process or machine." The religious concept of men in seeking to set up these relationships is anthropomorphic in the sense that the concept by which they set up relations with other men is anthropomorphic. In religion and in personal intercourse alike there is a postulate, namely, that there is in the material object which acts as nervous stimulus (*i.e.* the cosmos or the human body) that which is like our own power of self-direction, capacity for producing values, and personal response. On this hypothesis we treat the other as personal. But this requires some personal concept of the object to assist us in establishing interrelationship in a dynamic situation.

VI

The very exigencies of the behavior by which personal relations are expressed, therefore, demand that the word God should be more personal than an Absolute, or a Principle, or a personification of social values, or any other formula which does not include a possibility of personal response. The contribution which our experience makes to the term must be at the very frontier of our psychology, and our pattern must not belie our understanding of the cosmos. This is probably tantamount to saying that the pattern in our modern world will not be very sharply defined, but a term of emotion susceptible to rationalization. We pray as we love, not with a dictionary, but with an image. We stabilize ourselves in establishing this personal relation by a refusal to use methods or conceptions contradicting what our science tells us and by using such facts as science gives us. Like all personal relations, religion permits the use of figurative symbols as truly as poetry, for the symbol is not a definition but a psychological device for integrating dramatically one set of experiences with another. Different aspects of the same attitude can be expressed by different patterns, but personal pattern there must be if personal relations are to be established. Thus, while we should hesitate to speak of the metaphysical personality of God, he must always be thought of as personal, and as variously personal as the concept-making persons. In our endeavor to bring our behavior into relation with that which conditions us in the universe, we can use the analogy of father or great companion, or even the more ancient terms King and Almighty. The Christian will think of a Christ-like God. *For God is our conception, born of social experience, of the personality-evolving and personally responsive elements of our cosmic environment with which we are organically related.*

Particularly is this forming of psychological concepts necessary when in religion we utilize experience gained in establishing communication with other human beings as a method of coming into similar personal relations with the personally responsive elements of the cosmos. Prayer thus differs from meditation. Both alike have psychological value in religious behavior, but there is a fundamental difference between meditation and prayer. It is one which is recognized in our ordinary relations with persons. Consider the difference between thinking about a beloved friend and writing a love letter. The difference, in other words, is that prayer is a distinct effort, by the use of the psychological image, to organize a personal relationship by using a familiar mode of personal communication. Meditation, on the other hand, is the development of psychological states, which do not employ methods of conscious communication, although it may induce a state, as in the case of the mystic, which renders the self particularly susceptible to the personality-producing activities of the universe.

All this is an argument for a religious behavior akin to the means by which we set up personal relations with our fellows. And those means are forms of communication—language, symbolic acts, and the participation in group activity. In religion such forms of personal adjustment are prayer, religious ritual, and membership in a religious group. Such means of personal adjustment do not wait upon the intellect. They can be practiced by those whose conception of God may be cast in any pattern which makes such personal self-expression possible. The child, the simple-minded, may have very questionable conceptions of God, but they can live the religious life and get help from God. The only imperative need is that in such acts we do not violate our intellectual integrity.

VII

The fair question arises whether men in thus forming a personal concept of the personality-evolving and personally responsive activities of the universe as God must not logically hold to Satan as the conception of forces that cause suffering. There have been few religious movements in which this parallel process has not been carried on. Satan has been thought of as just as real and as personal as God, and to-day in orthodox Christianity he is distinctly recognized as a superhuman being who, having challenged the supremacy of God, has been cast down into hell, where with God's permission he eternally exercises his ingenuity in the punishment of the damned.

But such a being is not functional to the process of personal adjustment to the universe. He is an imaginary creature that will not endure scientific investigation. For he is the personification of impersonal, not personality-producing activity. It is the impersonal rather than the personality-evolving activities of the universe that bring suffering. Suffering results from forces of evolution that were, so far as our earth is concerned, prepersonal. They still continue after sentient organisms have been evolved. Long before there were any sentient beings on the planet there were volcanoes and storms and other activities of the physical world, but they produced no suffering, for inorganic matter cannot suffer. Suffering emerged when, thanks to the evolutionary process, there appeared forms superior to these physical forces. If such new forms of existence had no other power than that of suffering, one might well picture the process as evil. But as these new forms became personal they had the power of living in a plane out of the reach of impersonal forces. The evolutionary process, in producing this higher type of life which is personal, is an active reality and such of its elements as find expression in personalities must be treated as unavoidable elements in the environment in which such personalities must find self-expression and growth, and with which they must be adjusted. Impersonal forces cannot be so treated and one cannot come into personal relationship with them. The conception of Satan as a personal power of evil therefore violates the final test of the legitimacy of religious patterns. Our idea of God is our conception of personality-producing activity within our environment, but there is nothing except poetic personification of impersonal forces in the concept of Satan.

VIII

The pattern of organism in which we are beginning to think of God is both realistic and theistic. Its difference from conventional theism is that in the light of its history the term God is seen to involve psychological elements and is therefore not strictly metaphysical. It does, however, include also the reality of the cosmic activities capable of personal response. It thus can utilize, indeed must utilize, the appropriate data of science without being limited to the impersonal area of science. It avoids the difficulty attending the use of the term personality which, while applicable to men, has no meaning when raised to infinity. It also avoids the difficulties inherent in attempts to treat the universe psychologically, as if it were a human person raised to infinity. It does not say that the universe is either good or evil, but regards it as dynamic environment with which we must be intelligently adjusted. It is primarily religious rather than philosophical. If human endeavors to get into help-gaining adjustment with personally responsive activities of the universe are legitimate, one can without concern share in the discussion of metaphysicians as to whether the ultimate conception of the universe will be monistic. The belief that primordial activity had within itself the power of such combination and recombination as to bring forth conscious beings naturally argues that it must have within itself something akin to consciousness. But to debate the characteristics of the ultimate is as difficult as the theologians of the fourth century found the discussion of the Godhead before there was any universe. The human mind will never be content to abandon such discussions, for, like the Schoolmen, it demands some ultimate unity from which the various elements of experience may flow, but metaphysical discussion may easily pass beyond the area of experience represented by the word God. It is not the thing-in-itself with which religion deals, but that experience of organism in environment which makes a relationship with objective activities possible. A conceptual theism is more vital than a metaphysical theism, for its vanishing point is not an Absolute or a Principle or a Being, but personal relations with personality-creating, personally responsive, personally conceived activities of the cosmos. Such a conception of God is not exclusively metaphysical nor yet exclusively pragmatic. It favors neither pluralism nor a finite God. On the side of the concept, it is in the nature of the case pragmatic, but on the side of activities with which the pattern brings humanity into adjusted relationship it is metaphysical and as unlimited as the cosmos. It must, of course, be admitted that in so far as the term by its usage has within it a changing element of experience, it is not susceptible to fixed logical definition. But neither is any term which has to do with human experience. An existential infinite with which human experience comes into definite personal adjustment is scientifically demanded, but, as Thomas Aquinas said of the essence of God, "it lies beyond knowledge." But it is not beyond experience and human values. Like a vast parabola the personality-evolving activities of the cosmos touch our little circle of experience. We know not whence they come or whither they go, but we cannot evade them. We set up relations with them similar to those which we set up with persons. And thus we derive new strength and courage and moral motives for facing the tasks of life and building up a world-order in which personal relations will be more perfectly adjusted and human life happier. So long as this adjustment is made by the use of a theistic pattern, the value of the pattern will be determined on the one hand by its accord with such knowledge of the universe as we may possess, and on the other hand, by its capacity to further the personal values of life.

If the total activity of the universe is conceived of impersonally, as so many forces, if within it there can be discovered no tendencies that argue ends, then the idea of God will be incompatible with the universe. But no such

universe ever existed. If, on the other hand, the concept
of God be so sentimentalized as to lead men to hold that
the universe as a whole is statically good, men are likely
to be indifferent to the struggle involved in the process
toward larger personal values in which they are engaged.
Poverty and injustice are likely to be thought of as elements of a world which is the best possible in that it off-
sets discipline, suffering, sorrow, with the compensations
of a life to come. Lazarus may be licked by dogs in this
life, but in the life to come he rather than the rich man
will enjoy fellowship with Abraham.

Both of these conceptions, however, are to be rejected.
For, we repeat, human life is dependent upon a personality-producing process with which a man may choose to
adjust himself or be at enmity. He must struggle scientifically with the non-personal elements of the universe, but
his supreme aim is a richer personality, and a social order
which subordinates material goods to human values. In
this struggle he will be aided by science and by personal
adjustment with the cosmic activities which have made
human personality and human society possible. Therein
lies hope.

IX

The practical importance of this conceptual idea of God
is great. Representing in part, as the word does, that objective environment which expresses the ultimate reality
upon which human weal depends, it is bound to give more
than intellectual content to the mind-set. Man must
struggle scientifically with non-personal elements of the
universe and the backward pull of the vestiges of outgrown goods in both himself and society, but he can be
sure that he is not dependent solely upon his own efforts

or even on humanity's efforts. Humanity participates in an ongoing social process in which it is rendered more susceptible to the personality-evolving elements in the cosmic totality from which it came and in accordance with which it must live if it would grow more personal.

Morality has a religious basis in that the total process in which men are involved is toward personal values, and that any antipersonal activity is devolution, contrary to the primordial activity with which men are inexplicably involved. It is hard to see how anyone can fail to feel the worth of such a basis for morals. It is realism, not legalism. The God it recognizes is not a God of outgrown patterns but the intelligible cosmic activities within the realm of human situations. A given course of action is right if it is in accordance with the tendency of the process which has steadily differentiated personal from impersonal activities. This process may be described as the will of God, but such a description does not use the pattern of a sovereign but that of the relation of a personal organism with the personality-producing activities in the cosmic environment. To refuse to express and go on with the personality-producing, coördinating activities, to seek to live in a universe which has given birth to personality as if it were an impersonal machine, is to assure evil consequences. As gravitation will help a man if he build a wall plumb and oppose him if he build it out of plumb, so human beings who order their lives in accordance with these personality-producing activities we conceive as God, will build upon a rock. Not to live in harmony with them is to build upon sand.

Religion thus becomes more than conventional behavior. It is a technique by which the human being gains more personal value from personal adjustment with responsive cosmic activities. It would be difficult for any political or even parental conception of God to be regarded as expressing this conception accurately. It is more likely to be cast in the pattern of organic life itself, or the relations of the individual to the group. We can use both psychopathological patterns for the disintegration which comes from maladjustment to personal situations, and social psychology as a source of conceptions of the true relationship between the individual person and those cosmic activities which personally conceived respond to his personal approach. An exact definition of God is less basic than a directed adjustment to those cosmic activities which the word God represents.

x

We find integration and unity of experience whenever we undertake, by whatever personal concept is effective, to adjust our lives organically to a universe which is a source of physical sensation and in addition has the power to evoke a personal response on our part. With this personality-evoking activity we can enter into personal and help-gaining relationships. For such an adjustment the mystic has always stood. But so, to a greater or less extent, have all religions. Such a relationship has already been described as a bio-mysticism—the union on the plane of personality of a living organism with the environment upon which it depends.

Thus the outstanding fact which emerges from the history of the growth of the idea of God is that of a personal concept of the personally responsive activity in a cosmic environment from which humanity has come and upon which it is dependent. Though the content of the word God may be subject to social permutation, the per-

sonal organic relationship of men with environing activities as established by the use of some coördinating personal pattern, is as real as man's relationship with things
of sense. The conception of God is no more illusion than
the scientist's conception of the electron. Both are subject
to experimental validation. Men's tentative search for
cosmic adjustment and personal values conditioned by
such a concept need no more fear frustration than does the
adjustment of other aspects of our life to the imperfectly
understood but experientially accepted forces of electricity, gravitation, and light. In the struggles of life for
higher social and individual goods, men are enabled by
the use of a personal pattern to set up personal adjustment
with those personality-producing activities of the cosmos
by which they were evolved and on which they depend.
In such relation there is help and happiness. For we are
not comrades in doom but children of hope. We are
organically one with those cosmic activities we know as
God.

INDEX

Amos, 58, 74
Ancestor worship, 33
Angel of Jahweh, 71
Anselm, 152 *sq.*
Anthropomorphism, in Hebrew
    religion, 71; in human rela-
    tions, 223; in the idea of
    God, 224
Apocalypses, 79
Apuleius, 114
Aristotle, 98
Arius, 135
Arminianism, 172
Aryans, religion of, 93
Atheism, 212
Augustine, 138 *sq.;* and original
    sin, 147

Baalim, 52
Beelzebub, 80
Bernard of Clairvaux, 154, 158
Biomysticism, 233
Bruno, 165
Buddhism, 22, 130
Butler, 205

Calvinism, 171
Cappadocians, 137
Christianity, as a religion, 20 *sq.;*
    and primitive peoples, 40
Cleianthes, hymn of, 106
Confucianism, 22
Covenant, 173
Cynic philosophy, 104

Day of judgment, 84
Dead, fear of, 31
Deism, 173, 190
Democracy, theological influence
    of, 174 *sq.*

Devil, 160
Dispersion, 75, **118**

Eddington, 197 *sq.*
Emperor worship, 101 *sq.*
Epictetus, 1, 104, 109, 111
Epicurean idea of God, 100
Erigena, 149
Eucken, 202
Ezekiel, 85

Fear, not the origin of the idea
    of God, 34
Fourth Gospel, Jesus of, 124
Francis of Assisi, 159

Gnosticism, 128
God, definition of, 226
    idea of, 11, 39, 62; outgrowth
        of religious behavior, 3, 225;
        expressed in patterns of
        primitive life, 28, nomadic
        life, 49, agricultural life, 51,
        national life, 54, international
        life, 60, feudal pattern, 152;
        as father, 83, 85, 179; as
        imperial sovereign, 144 *sq.*,
        147, 150; as Absolute, 98,
        205; as principle, 204, 207;
        as creditor, 176
God, idea of, as instrumental,
        220; as involving both ex-
        perience and cosmic activ-
        ities 212 *sq.;* modified by so-
        cial customs, 13 *sq.*, 18, 35,
        37; affected by the Renais-
        sance, 163; affected by sci-
        ence, 183; among the Greeks
        —according to Socrates, 96,
        Plato, 97, Aristotle, 98, Stoics,

235

100; in Gnosticism, 130;
Trinity, 131; teaching of
Paul, 89; teaching of Thomas
Aquinas, 154 *sq.;* as national
sovereign, 168; as constitutional sovereign, 173; pattern
of organism, 222
technique of adjustment with,
226
Gods, origin of, 34; and mores,
38
Greeks, original religion of, 94;
rise of religious philosophy
among, 94; Socrates, 96;
Platonism, 97

Hebrew religion, early monothe-
ism, 57; connection with
other religions, 47; anthro-
pomorphism in 71; polythe-
ism in, 64, 70 *sq.*
Hebrews, origin of religion of,
44 *sq.*
Hinduism, 22, 23, 130
Holy Roman Empire, 151
Hosea, 59
Humanism, 193 *sq.*
Huxley, J. S., 201

Idols, 37; explanation of, 107
Imperialism, influence in theol-
ogy, 150
Isaiah, 61

Jahweh, first recognized, 48; in
the pattern of nomadic life,
49; becomes God of agriculture, 52; of a nation, 54;
residence of, 55; international
affairs, 60; as creator, 63;
moral authority, 66, 76; military character of, 66; character of, 67; anthropomor-
phically described, 71; and
abode of the dead, 62, 72;
in the pattern of Oriental
sovereign, 74; in the apocalypses, 79; persistence of
Hebrew idea of, 90
James, 205

Jeans, 199
Jeremiah, 68, 85
Jesus, and the messianic hope, 81;
regarded as divine, 88,
121 *sq.,* 126 *sq.,* 140, 181;
teaching as to God, 83

Lodge, Sir Oliver, 200
Logos, 100
Lutheranism, 170

Magic, 32
Magicians, among Jews, 75
Maimonides, 154
Mana, 28
Mary, hyperdulia of, 162, 180
Maximus of Tyre, 107
Messianic hope, 78, 81
Micah, 59, 69
Millikan, 199
Mithra, 113
Monotheism, Christian, chap. 5;
of the Greeks, 94 *sq.;* of the
Hebrews, 90
Morality, as based in religion,
232
Morgan, 199
Mystery, as distinguished from
the unknown, 28
Mystery religions, nature of,
111 *sq.;* and Paul, 123
Mysticism, 148, 158

Nazarites, 74
Neoplatonism, 158

Origen, 136
Otto, M. C., 203

Patterns, origin of, 7; and religion, 9; nature of, 25; values
expressed in, 208; summary
of, 210; of organism, 228
Paul, doctrine of God, 89; faith
in Jesus, 121; and mystery
religions, 123
Personæ, 134
Philo, 73, 75
Platonism, 97
Plutarch, 108